The Giant American History Timeline

Book 2
1870s–Present

Sunflower education

★ TABLE OF CONTENTS ★

INTRODUCTION

TIMELINE COMPONENTS

★ Unit 1 ★ Industrial Growth and Technological Advancement: 1870–1910

TEACHING NOTES

ACTIVITY SHEETS

★ Unit 2 ★ Big Business and Social Reform: 1870–1910

★ Unit 3 ★ America and the World: 1867–1910

★ Unit 6 ★ World War II: 1930–1950

★ Unit 7 ★ The Cold War: 1940–1990

★ Unit 8 ★ The Civil Rights Movement, Technology, and Terrorism: 1954–Present

★ Assessments ★

★ Answer Key ★

★ Introduction ★

Most parents/teachers are all too familiar with students who can recite facts without understanding them within a historical context. *The Giant American History Timeline 2* is designed to give students an overall understanding of American history. Specific facts make sense to students when presented within a larger context.

The unique approach used in *The Giant American History Timeline 2* makes American history accessible for students of varying ages and abilities. Your students will enjoy researching and presenting facts about significant events, people, and places in American history while completing the high-interest activity sheets in each unit. Students will then help you create a detailed timeline to display in the classroom or hallway. As students progress through the program, they will modify and expand the timeline so that it progresses with them.

The timeline approach allows students to see how much they have learned as their work is displayed and provides them with an organized, ongoing review of the material presented. Students will work individually and in groups to create visual presentations they can prominently and proudly display.

The Giant American History Timeline 2 will allow you to:

- create detailed timelines for specific periods in American history;
- customize the timelines to meet your students' needs;
- use the timelines to help students understand historical patterns; and
- emphasize students' development of essential critical thinking skills.

While completing activity sheets and assembling timelines, students will practice critical thinking skills such as identifying main ideas and details, sequencing events, and relating causes and effects. For students to have a solid understanding of history, they must be able to understand what happened (main ideas and details), when it happened (sequencing), and how the event relates to other things that happened (cause and effect).

This program involves students in asking questions about historical events, people, and places while guiding them to develop a complete understanding of American history.

How *The Giant American History Timeline 2* Is Organized

Two Books

This book is the second in a series of two. Book 1 covers the arrival of early peoples in North America through Reconstruction. Book 2 begins with the industrial growth and technological advancements after Reconstruction and covers American history through the present.

Units

This reproducible, 234-page book consists of eight units that introduce students to the period after Reconstruction through the present. Units include:

Unit 1. Industrial Growth and Technological Advancement: 1870–1910

Unit 2. Big Business and Social Reform: 1870–1910

Unit 3. America and the World: 1867–1910

Unit 4. World War I: 1910–1920

Unit 5. The Roaring Twenties and the Great Depression: 1920–1940

Unit 6. World War II: 1930–1950

Unit 7. The Cold War: 1940–1990

Unit 8. The Civil Rights Movement, Technology, and Terrorism: 1954–Present

Units 1, 2, and 3 cover the same historical period, but each focuses on a different topic related to the period. Units 4, 5, 6, 7, and 8 each address a different historical period. Each unit includes a Teaching Notes section, followed by 15 or 16 student activity sheets.

Teaching Notes

The Teaching Notes section in each unit includes the following:

Unit Overview—an overview of the major historical developments of the period and how they are addressed on the activity sheets

Focus Activities—three activities that focus students' attention on the period being studied

Constructing the Timeline—instructions for assembling completed activity sheets to form a classroom timeline; provides diagrams for creating a basic timeline or a complete timeline

Critical Thinking Skills—a description of the critical thinking skills reinforced in the unit, both by the activity sheets and the completed timeline

Individual Activity Sheet Notes—specific instructions on guiding students through the completion and extension of each activity sheet

Activity Sheets

The activity sheets are presented in a variety of formats to make them appropriate for students of varying ability levels and learning styles and to ensure that the posted timelines are visually appealing. Students will create and complete maps, complete and extend graphic organizers, analyze primary source materials, answer questions, write captions, create graphs, compare and contrast time periods, and more.

In every unit, each activity sheet is labeled with a number and a letter that identify the unit number as well as the activity's placement within the unit. For example, the first activity sheet in Unit 1 is labeled 1-A. The activity sheets are presented in chronological order.

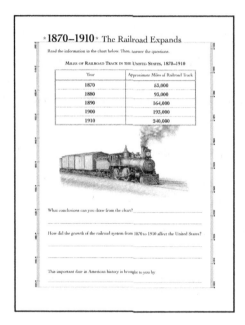

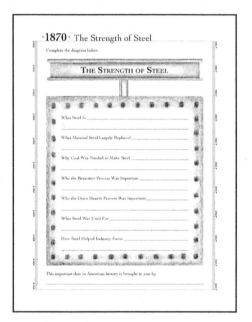

Six types of activity sheets are repeated throughout the program. These activity sheets provide historical continuity and visual cohesion within the posted timelines.

Title Activity Sheets

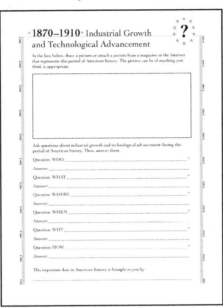

The first activity sheet in every unit has the same title as the unit in which it appears. As students complete these activity sheets, they generate and answer general questions about the historical periods being covered. The eight Title Activity Sheets feature the titles and main ideas of the historical periods on the posted timelines.

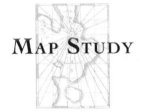

Map Study Activity Sheets

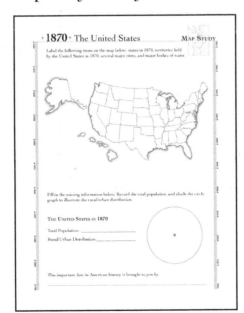

These activity sheets appear in various places within the units. Students complete a map of the United States and analyze the U.S. population during certain time periods.

BIOGRAPHY

Biography Activity Sheets

These activity sheets appear in various places within the units. Biography Activity Sheets focus on one or more significant people from the historical period being covered.

A VOICE FROM THE PAST

A Voice From the Past Activity Sheets

These activity sheets appear in various places within the units. A Voice From the Past Activity Sheets provide students with high-interest primary source materials from the historical periods being covered.

Time Machine Activity Sheets

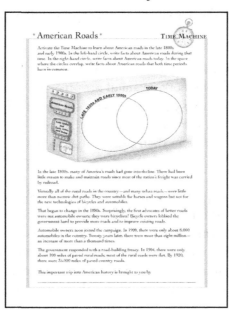

The next-to-last activity sheet in every unit addresses a high-interest social history topic. Students "set" the Time Machine to a certain topic and time period (for example, American roads during the late 1800s and early 1900s) and read the mini-essay provided on the activity sheet. Then, students compare and contrast information about that topic during the time period addressed with the same topic today.

A Postcard From the Past Activity Sheets

The last activity sheet in every unit directs students to research a notable, unit-related historical site in the United States and create a postcard to "send" from that place.

USING THE ACTIVITY SHEETS

The includes 125 activity sheets that vary in topic, format, and difficulty. In every unit, suggestions for clarifying and extending the topics covered on each activity sheet are provided under the Individual Activity Sheet Notes category in the Teaching Notes section.

As your students work through the activity sheets, keep the following guidelines in mind:

Assigning Activity Sheets

You may assign the activity sheets in any way you see fit. Students can complete each activity sheet individually, with partners, in small groups, or as a whole class. Please note that the name line at the bottom of each activity sheet is designed to give the students "classroom credit" when their work is posted as part of a timeline and to encourage the students to take pride in their accomplishments.

Completing Activity Sheets

Most activity sheets in *Giant* require students to conduct research in order to complete them. The amount and intensity of research required varies. In some cases, students must simply recall information from class discussions or consult their textbooks to find basic facts; in other cases, students must conduct library or Internet research. After the students complete an activity sheet, encourage them to use colored pencils to shade the illustrations and maps, which will make the displayed timelines more visually appealing.

Modifying Activity Sheets

Encourage students to modify the activity sheets in appropriate ways. For example, students can add indicator lines and additional cells to graphic organizers to incorporate specific things they learned in class. They can write additional questions and the answers they find. Students can also add illustrations as appropriate.

Extending Activity Sheets

Each activity sheet can be extended in a variety of ways, such as participating in follow-up discussions, expanding graphic organizers, and conducting additional research.

UNIT ASSESSMENTS

A two-page unit assessment is provided for each unit. All eight assessments are located in the last section of the book. The first page of each assessment contains objective items and is designed to function as a basic assessment. This page focuses on the critical thinking skills of identifying main ideas and details as well as sequencing events. The second page features two short, subjective essay questions that are more difficult. One question addresses the critical thinking skill of relating causes and effects, while the other question asks students to express an opinion. You may assign the first page only for lower-level students or both pages for higher-level students.

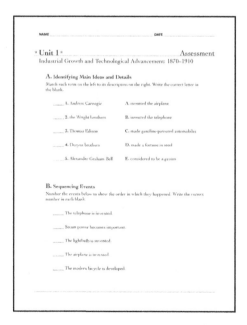

CREATING TIMELINES

The timelines created with *American* consist of two basic parts: the activity sheets, completed by students, and the Timeline Components, which connect the activity sheets to form coherent timelines.

Creating timelines with *History* is a simple, three-step process:

> **Step 1. Design the Timeline** The Teaching Notes section at the beginning of each unit provides two suggested timelines: a basic timeline (using just a few activity sheets in the unit) and a complete timeline (using all of the activity sheets in the unit). You may choose to create either one of these timelines or design your own customized timeline.

> **Step 2. Assign the Activity Sheets** Assign the activity sheets that you want to include in the timeline. Guide students as they complete the activity sheets.

> **Step 3. Construct the Timeline** Assemble the timeline on a classroom or hallway wall, attaching the activity sheets with push pins, tape, or removable adhesive.

Student Participation

The level of student participation in creating timelines is up to you, but all three steps outlined above are amenable to student input and even student control. For example, you might guide students as they design a timeline or even assign them the task of designing the timeline themselves.

Using the Timeline Arrows

The Timeline Arrows are used to connect and show relationships among the events, people, and places that are the topics of the activity sheets. The Timeline Arrows are provided on page XVIII.

Historical Relationships and Critical Thinking

By positioning the arrows judiciously, it is easy to give students a sense of the connections among the activity sheet topics and reinforce the critical thinking skills of identifying main ideas and details, sequencing events, and relating causes and effects. Use formats similar to the ones shown in the diagrams on the next two pages to emphasize these critical thinking skills when creating timelines. Each rectangle represents a completed activity sheet, and each arrow represents a Timeline Arrow sheet.

Identifying Main Ideas and Details

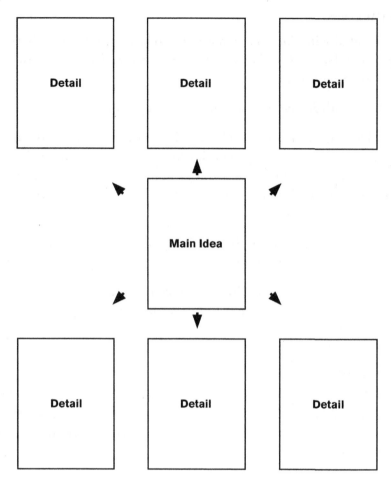

Sequencing Events

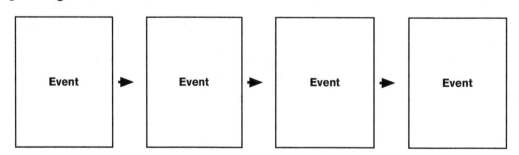

Relating Causes and Effects

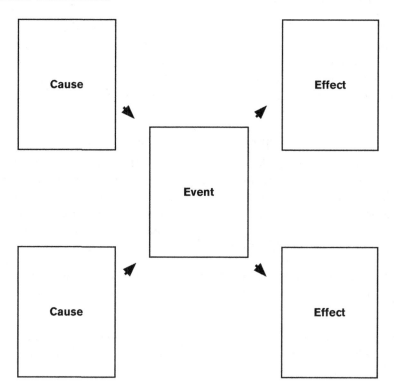

Annotating the Timeline Arrows

Write words and phrases on the Timeline Arrows to clarify what they represent. For example, you might write such phrases as, "was followed by," "resulted in," and "was a main cause of," to help make the timeline more readable and the topics of the individual activity sheets less discrete. You might also direct students to color or illustrate the Timeline Arrows appropriately.

Using the Timeline Dates

The Timeline Dates are used to provide a temporal background for the events, people, and places that are the topics of the activity sheets. The Timeline Dates are provided on pages XIX–XXII.

The Timeline Dates are in ten-year intervals. Page XIX includes a blank Timeline Date space to accommodate any specific need you might have.

Using the Timeline Subheadings

A Title Activity Sheet provides a title for the timeline created by each unit. In addition, the timelines created by Units 1, 2, and 5 can incorporate subheadings. The subheadings for these units are provided on pages XXIII–XXV. The boxes are for student illustrations.

★ Research and Standards ★

The National Council for the Social Studies (NCSS) synthesized the "findings from the best available classroom research" and identified "an emerging consensus of expert opinion about how to teach social studies." The result is a vision for "powerful teaching and learning in the social studies," in which "powerful" refers to "ideal forms of social studies teaching and learning." According to the NCSS, social studies teaching and learning are powerful when they are: meaningful, integrative, value-based, challenging, and active.

The Giant American History Timeline 2 supports each of these key elements:

Meaningful This book creates networks—the timelines—that give meaning to American history. The NCSS writes, "Facts and ideas are not taught in isolation from other content, nor are skills. Instead, they are embedded in networks of knowledge, skills, beliefs, and attitudes that are structured around important ideas and taught emphasizing their connections.... New topics are framed with reference to where they fit within the big picture ... content is developed in ways that help students see how its elements relate to one another (e.g., using ... graphic learning aids ...)."

Integrates This book integrates knowledge of discrete historical events within the timelines. The NCSS writes, "Powerful social studies teaching is integrative across time and space, connecting with past experience ...."

Value-Based This book exposes students to different points of view about historical events in various activity sheets. The NCSS writes, "Powerful social studies teaching encourages recognition of opposing points of view ...."

Challenges This book provides appropriate individual challenges in activity sheets and fosters collaborative learning as students combine the sheets to construct the timelines. The NCSS writes, "Students ... strive to accomplish instructional goals both as individuals and as group members ... Students ... respond thoughtfully to one another's ideas."

Actively This book lets students actively construct timelines that form a network of understanding about American history. The NCSS writes, "Students develop new understanding through a process of construction. They do not passively receive or copy curriculum content ... they strive to make sense of what they are learning by developing a network of connections that link the new content to preexisting knowledge ...."

The Giant American History Timeline 2 meets both state and NCSS national social studies standards. As students construct the timelines, they will fulfill major aspects of all major social studies strands identified by the NCSS.

- Strand I: Culture
- Strand II: Time, Continuity, and Change
- Strand III: People, Places, and Environments
- Strand IV: Individual Development and Identity
- Strand V: Individuals, Groups, and Institutions
- Strand VI: Power, Authority, and Governance
- Strand VII: Production, Distribution, and Consumption
- Strand VIII: Science, Technology, and Society
- Strand IX: Global Connections

"A Vision of Powerful Teaching and Learning in the Social Studies." Silver Spring, Maryland: NCSS. 1994.

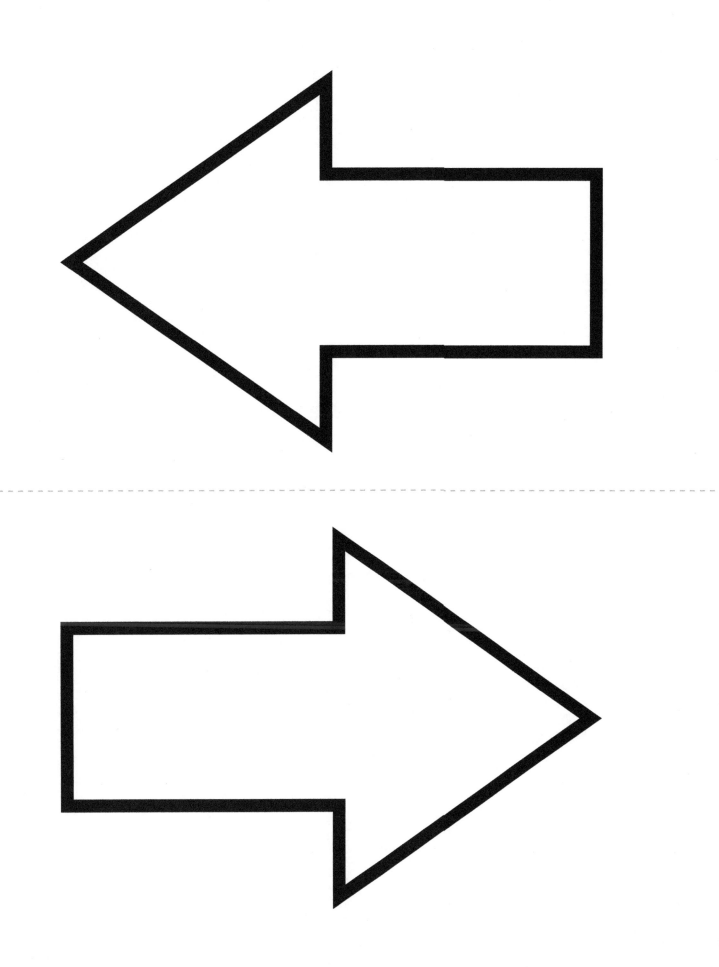

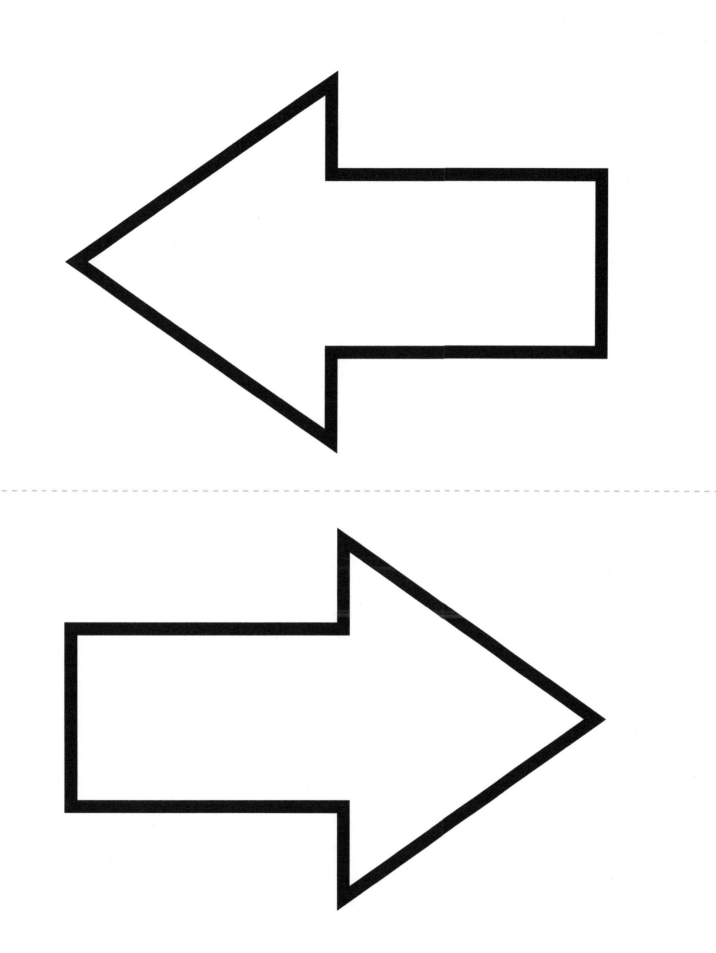

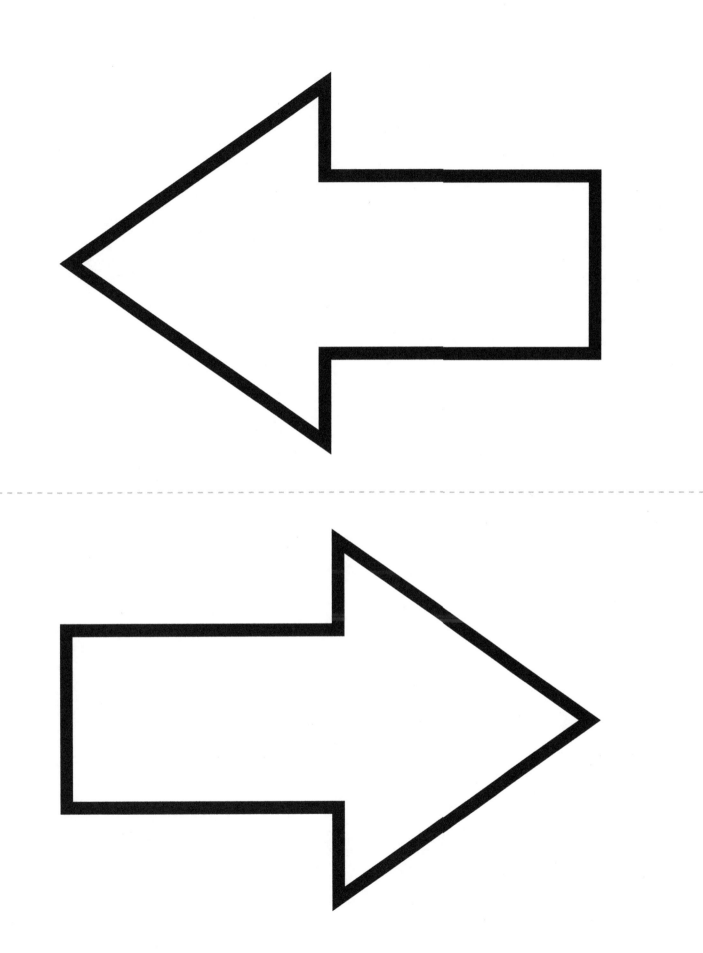

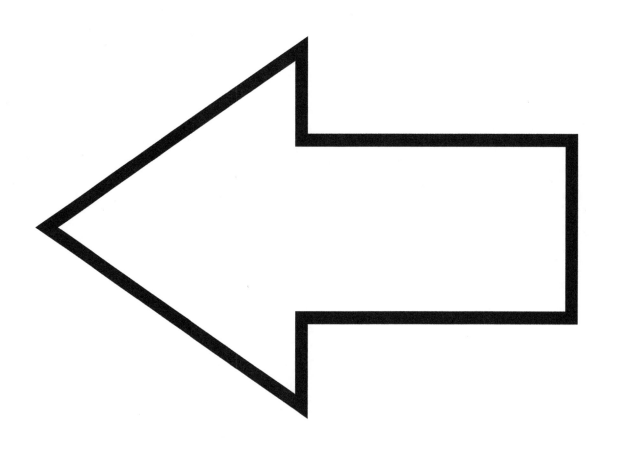
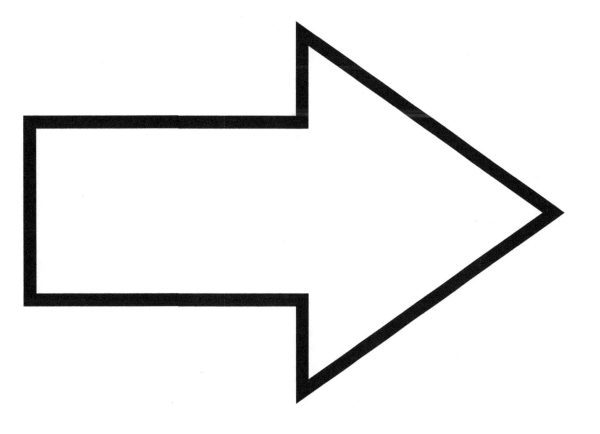

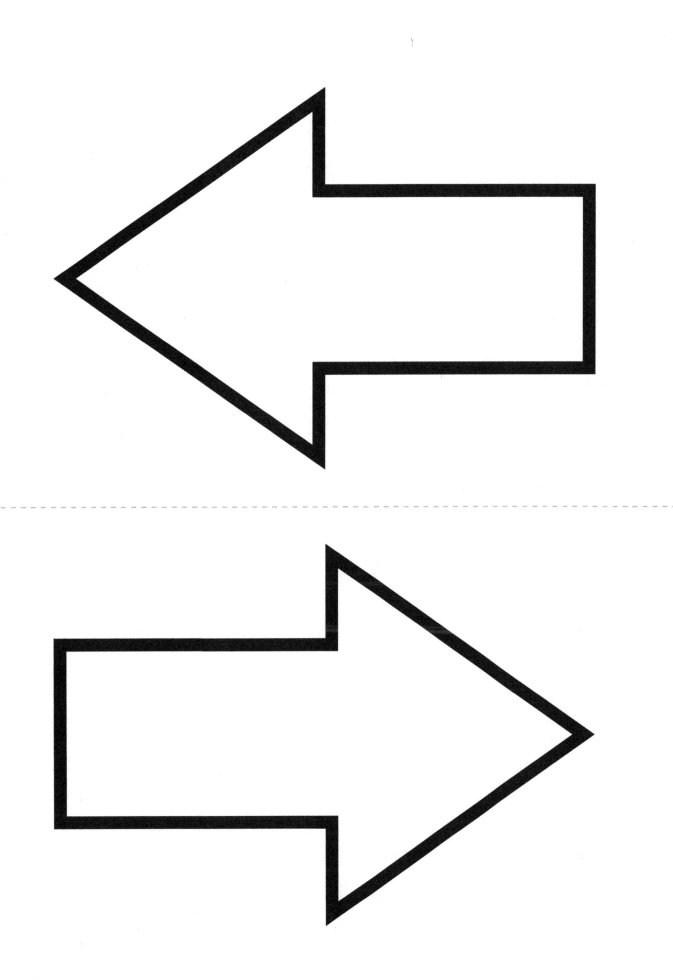

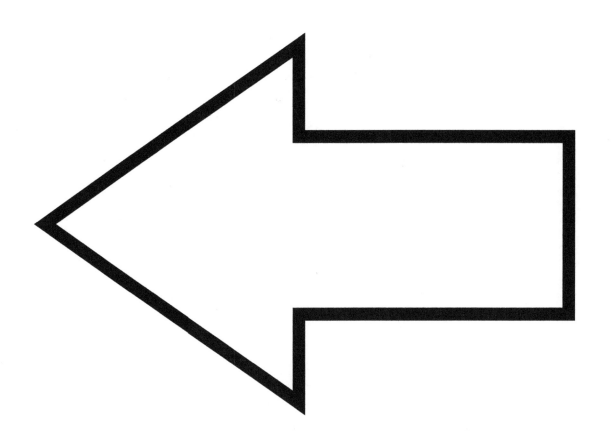
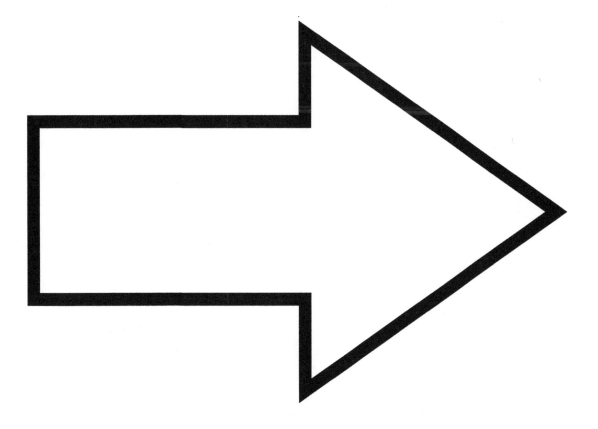

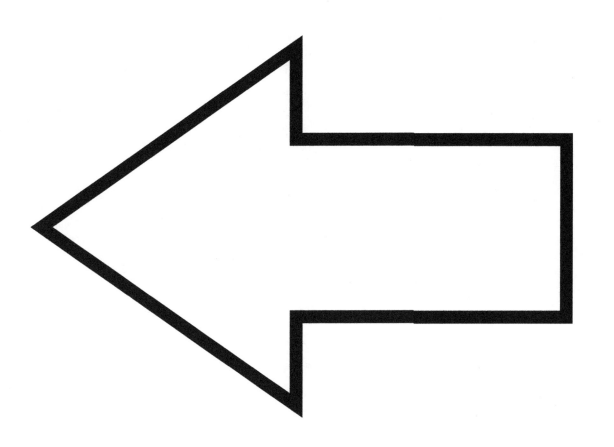

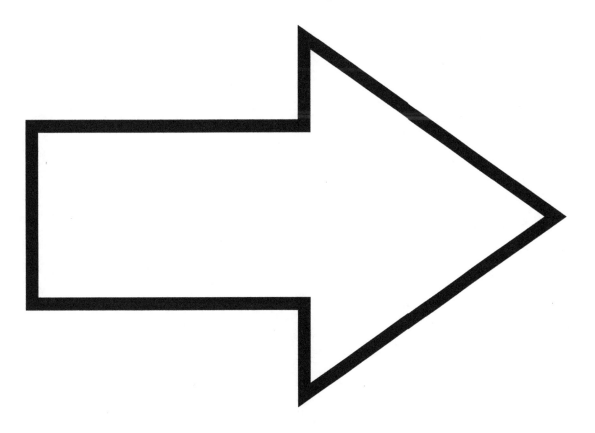

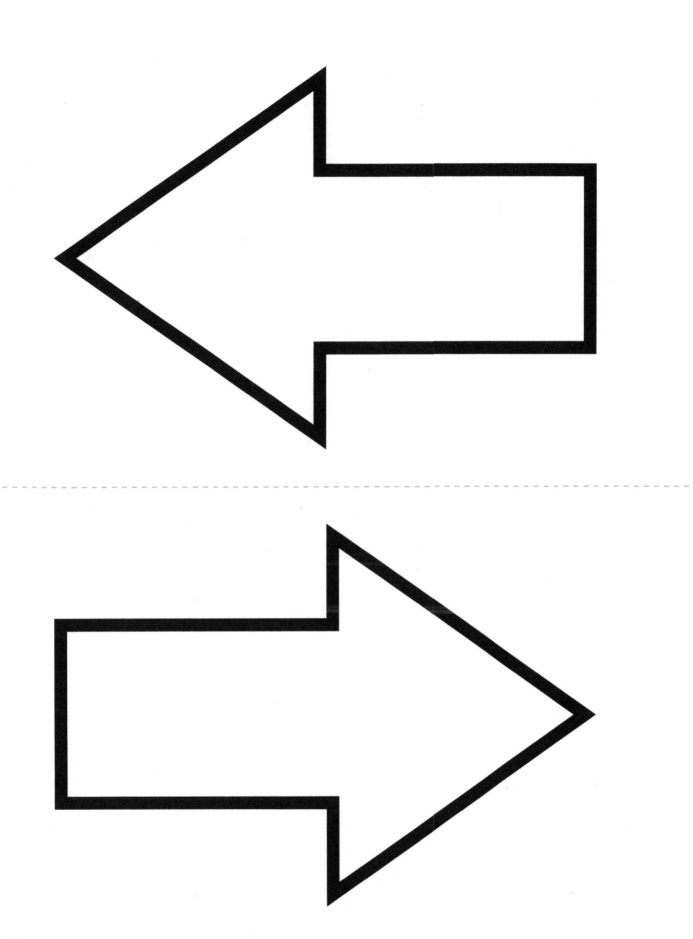

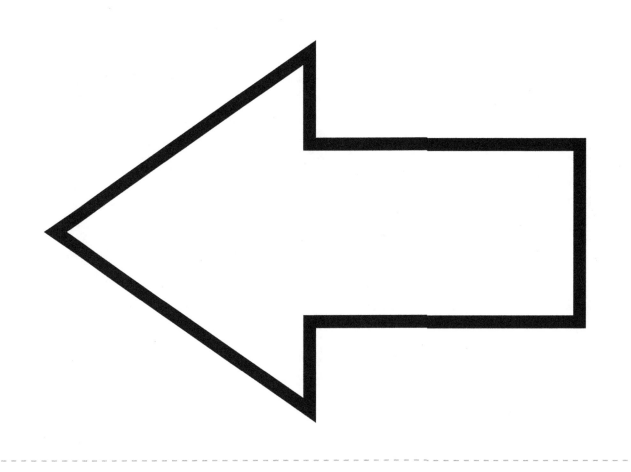
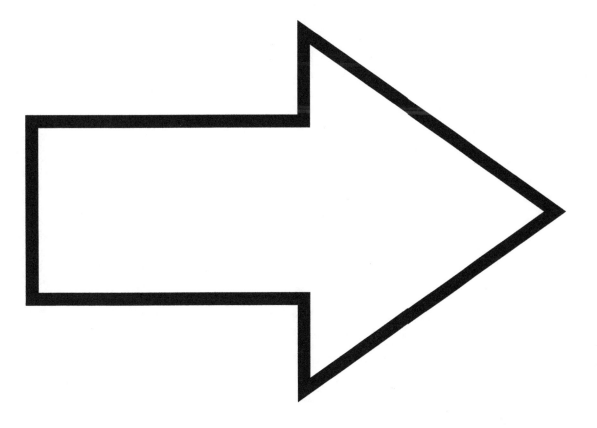

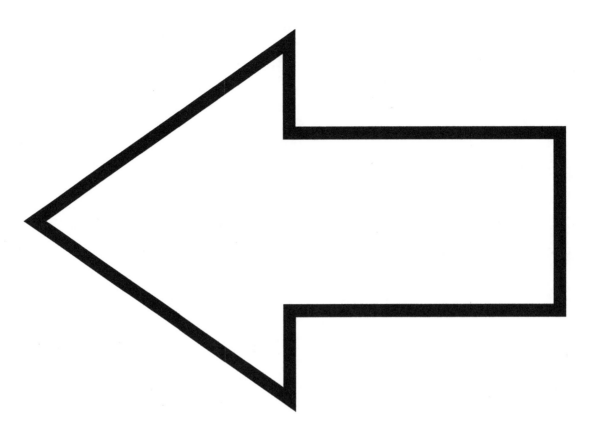
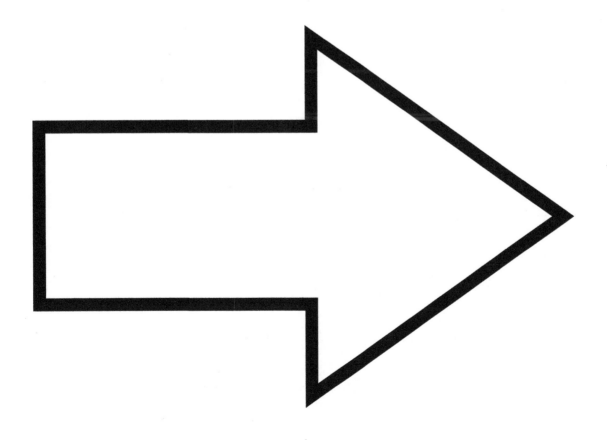

1870

1880

1890

1900

1910

1920

1930

1940

1950

1960

1970

1980

1990

2000

2010

2020

2030

THE HARD LIVES OF WORKERS

ATTEMPTS AT REFORM

THE ROARING TWENTIES

INDUSTRIALIZATION

NEW TECHNOLOGY

THE POWER OF BIG BUSINESS

THE GREAT DEPRESSION

UNIT 1   Industrial Growth and Technological Advancement

1870–1910

UNIT OVERVIEW

The story of America in the late nineteenth and early twentieth centuries is largely the story of industrial and technological achievement. The country became an industrial powerhouse during this period, and many technological advances and inventions that radically altered the way people lived emerged during this time.

Unit 1 focuses on this industrial and technological advancement. Units 2 and 3 address other historical developments during this time period.

Activity Sheet 1-A provides a unit overview. Activity Sheet 1-B sets the geopolitical and demographic stage for this period of American history. Activity Sheets 1-C through 1-F focus on industrialization, including three key factors in the growth of industry—the railroad, steel, and steam power.

Activity Sheets 1-G through 1-L focus on the amazing new personalities and technologies that shaped the era. The telephone is the subject of Activity Sheet 1-H. Activity Sheet 1-I examines the life of Thomas Edison. Activity Sheets 1-J, 1-K, and 1-L focus on the inventions of the bicycle, the automobile, and the airplane. Activity Sheet 1-M provides a view of the country at the turn of the century.

The Time Machine, Activity Sheet 1-N, compares American roads today to American roads in the late nineteenth and early twentieth centuries. A Postcard From the Past, Activity Sheet 1-O, is about the Wright Brothers National Memorial.

FOCUS ACTIVITIES

To focus the students' attention on this period of American history, consider the following activities:

Imagine Life Without

Discuss some of the remarkable inventions created during this period of American history (for example, the light bulb, the telephone, and the airplane). Ask the students how their lives might be different if these things did not exist.

A Genius at Work

Ask the students what they know about Thomas Edison. Record their responses on the board. Explain that he is considered to be a genius but that he himself said, "Genius is one percent inspiration and ninety-nine percent perspiration." Challenge the students to explain the meaning of this statement.

Second Industrial Revolution

Ask the students what they know about the Industrial Revolution. Explain that many historians consider the growth of American industry in the late nineteenth century to be a second Industrial Revolution. Discuss this opinion with the students.

CONSTRUCTING THE TIMELINE

This unit consists of 15 activity sheets that focus on significant events, people, and places related to industrial growth and technological advancement during the late nineteenth and early twentieth centuries. Each activity sheet is designed to, once completed, become part of a posted classroom timeline of the period covered in the unit.

The Introduction (pages VII–XIII) provides a detailed explanation of how to use the activity sheets in the classroom and suggests various ways to construct the timeline u sing the completed activity sheets.

You can construct the timeline any way you see fit. Use the Timeline Components (pages XVIII–XXV) to connect the activity sheets. Below are two possible timelines, constructed from the activity sheets in this unit and the Timeline Components.

Option 1: Basic Timeline
Construct this timeline to identify only the essential elements of the period.

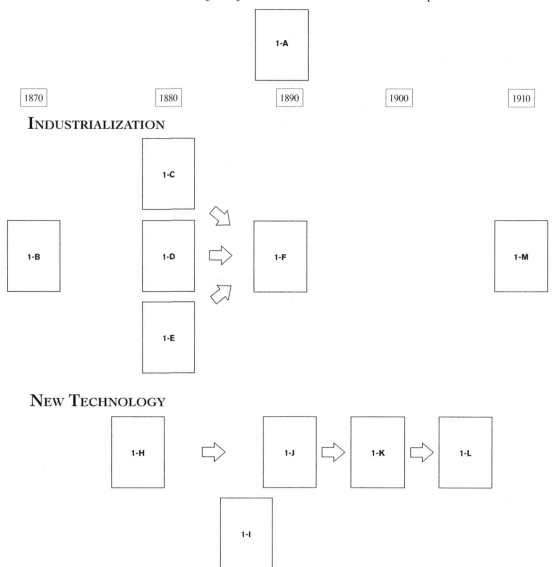

Option 2: Complete Timeline

Construct this timeline to identify the essential elements of the period, examine them in greater detail, and extend student learning.

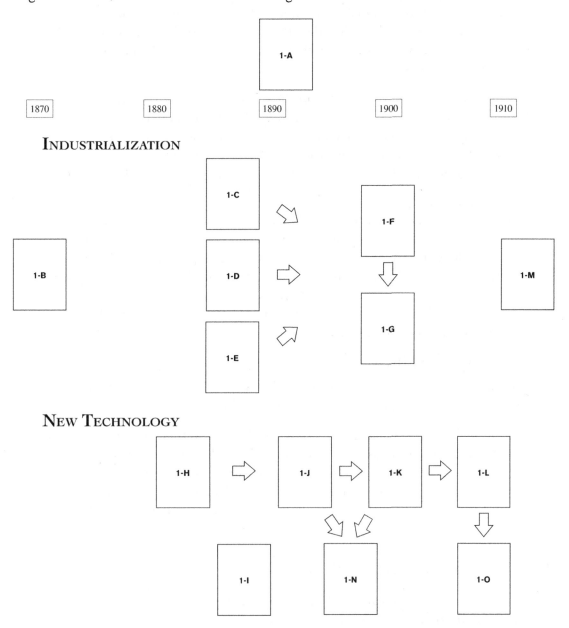

CRITICAL THINKING SKILLS

The activity sheets in this unit address various critical thinking skills. In addition, the constructed timeline emphasizes the essential critical thinking skills of identifying main ideas and details, sequencing events, and relating causes and effects.

Identifying Main Ideas and Details

Make sure the students understand the concepts of main idea and details. Explain that a main idea is a broad topic while details provide specific information about the main idea. Point out that Activity Sheet 1-A outlines the main ideas of the unit. Explain that the other activity sheets in the unit reflect the main ideas of the historical period the students are studying. Further explain that some activity sheets focus on the details related to specific topics.

As you and the students construct the timeline, show them that the first subheading is a main idea while Activity Sheets 1-B through 1-G focus on details. Point out the similar relationship between the second subheading and Activity Sheets 1-H through 1-L. Have the students annotate the Timeline Arrows appropriately. Challenge the students to find similar relationships or create them by rearranging the activity sheets.

Sequencing Events

Point out that the activity sheets that make up the timeline are sequential. Show the students how the Timeline Dates provide a concrete reference for when events happened and how they relate to other events. (For example, the first American gasoline automobile plant was opened in 1895 before the airplane was invented in 1903.) Make sure the students see that the Timeline Arrows indicate a chronological flow from left to right. Also, remind the students that this unit's timeline has two basic layers that are separated by subheadings.

Relating Causes and Effects

Explain the relationship between a cause and an effect. Point out that there can be multiple causes and/or multiple effects in any situation.

As you and the students construct the timeline, show them that Activity Sheets 1-C through 1-E focus on the causes of the effect addressed on Activity Sheet 1-F. Point out that Activity Sheets 1-J and 1-K discuss the causes of the effect described on Activity Sheet 1-N. Have the students annotate the Timeline Arrows appropriately. Challenge the students to find similar relationships or create them by rearranging the activity sheets.

INDIVIDUAL ACTIVITY SHEET NOTES

The notes below provide a variety of tips on how to guide the students through the completion and extension of each activity sheet.

1-A. Industrial Growth and Technological Advancement

This activity is most appropriate for the students to complete with partners, in small groups, or as a whole class. For example, you might want to complete the questions with the whole class at the beginning of the unit and then have the students answer the questions at the end of the unit. Encourage the students to think of additional questions related to the topic.

1-B. Map Study: The United States in 1870

Remind the students that the Civil War was just five years in the past, that Reconstruction was in full swing, and that the map is of a country still healing from a great rift.

1-C. The Railroad Expands

Make sure the students understand that the expansion of the railroad relied on coal (to make steel and to fire locomotives). Emphasize the dramatic effect this nationwide, efficient, high-speed network for carrying goods and people had on the economic and social climates of the United States.

1-D. The Strength of Steel

Point out that coal was a necessity for making steel. Explain that although this metal had been developed much earlier, the new steel-making process produced a much better quality of steel and produced it much more efficiently. Emphasize that steel was needed for the railroad system—for rails, railroad cars, and locomotives.

1-E. Steam Powers the Nation

Point out that coal was needed for steam engines, both to make the steel used to create vital engine parts and to fire the boilers. Consider bringing a working model steam engine to class to demonstrate how impressive steam engines once were because of the amount of power they generated.

1-F. American Industry Booms

Emphasize the wide-ranging effects of industrial development on the world, including natural resources, workers, business organization, business-government organization, and international relations.

1-G. A Voice From the Past: Andrew Carnegie

Invite an interested student to give a book report on an appropriate biography about Carnegie. Ask the student to explain Carnegie's views of wealth and philanthropy. Discuss the Carnegie endowments, as well as the many public institutions in the United States today that bear his name.

1-H. The Telephone

Allow interested students to research Alexander Graham Bell's fascinating life in more detail. In addition to inventing the telephone, he also worked to help deaf people communicate, invented a metal detector, experimented with kites, helped found the National Geographic Society, and raced speedboats.

1-I. Biography: Thomas Edison

Edison, the quintessential American genius, was known for his work ethic. Take this opportunity to emphasize the value of hard work and dedication.

1-J. The Bicycle

Make sure the students understand that bicyclists, more than drivers, were the first champions of better roads. Consider conducting a debate in class on the merits of bicycles as primary transportation devices versus automobiles. (For example, bicycles promote physical health, they do not pollute the air, and they are quiet.)

1-K. The Automobile

Select a few students to conduct additional research about the automobile in American life today, including the average number of cars per household, the average number of miles driven per year, and the number of miles of roadway in the United States. Emphasize the fundamental impact the automobile has had on American civilization.

1-L. The Airplane

Share with the students a fact so obvious that it is usually overlooked: When Orville Wright first flew, he didn't know how to pilot an airplane!

1-M. Map Study: The United States in 1900

Have the students compare and contrast this map with the map on Activity Sheet 1-B. Emphasize the growing population of the United States and its increasing urbanization.

1-N. Time Machine: American Roads

Help the students identify the main points of the essay, which should be written in the left-hand circle of the Venn diagram.

1-O. A Postcard From the Past: Wright Brothers National Memorial

Suggest that the students visit www.nps.gov (the web site of the National Park Service) to gather information about the Wright Brothers National Memorial.

★ 1870–1910 ★ Industrial Growth and Technological Advancement

In the box below, draw a picture or attach a picture from a magazine or the Internet that represents this period of American history. The picture can be of anything you think is appropriate.

Ask questions about industrial growth and technological advancement during this period of American history. Then, answer them.

Question: WHO_____?

Answer:_____

Question: WHAT_____?

Answer:_____

Question: WHERE _____?

Answer:_____

Question: WHEN _____?

Answer:_____

Question: WHY_____?

Answer:_____

Question: HOW_____?

Answer:_____

This important date in American history is brought to you by

_____

Label the following items on the map below: states in 1870, territories held by the United States in 1870, several major cities, and major bodies of water.

Fill in the missing information below. Record the total population, and shade the circle graph to illustrate the rural/urban distribution.

THE UNITED STATES IN 1870

Total Population: _____

Rural/Urban Distribution:_____

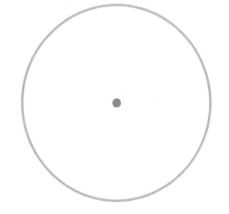

This important date in American history is brought to you by

_____

Read the information in the chart below. Then, answer the questions.

MILES OF RAILROAD TRACK IN THE UNITED STATES, 1870–1910

Year	Approximate Miles of Railroad Track
1870	53,000
1880	93,000
1890	164,000
1900	193,000
1910	240,000

What conclusions can you draw from the chart? _____

_____

How did the growth of the railroad system from 1870 to 1910 affect the United States?

_____

_____

This important date in American history is brought to you by

_____

Complete the diagram below.

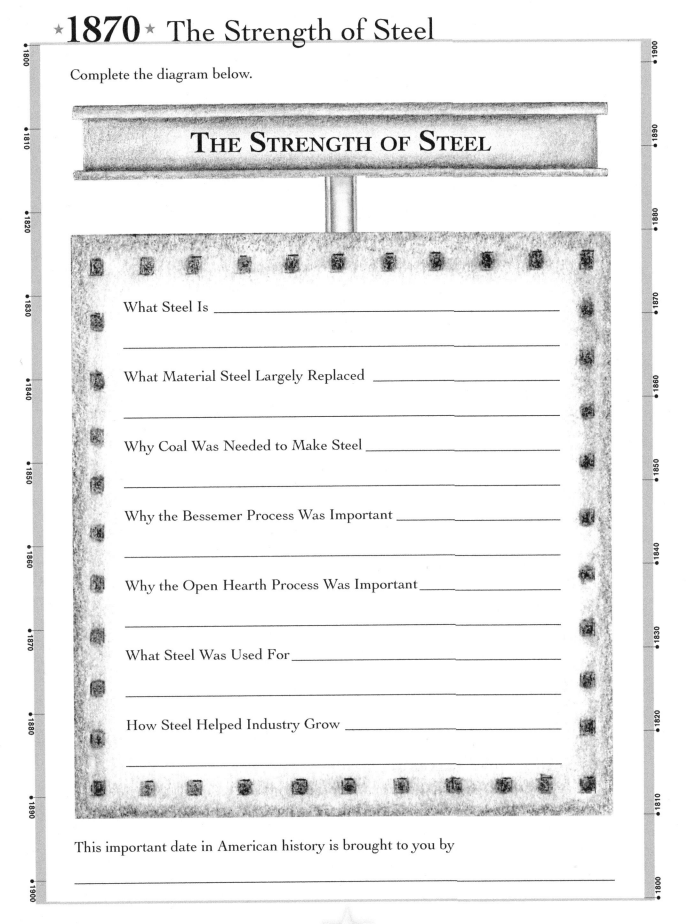

THE STRENGTH OF STEEL

What Steel Is _____

_____

What Material Steel Largely Replaced _____

_____

Why Coal Was Needed to Make Steel _____

_____

Why the Bessemer Process Was Important _____

_____

Why the Open Hearth Process Was Important _____

_____

What Steel Was Used For _____

_____

How Steel Helped Industry Grow _____

_____

This important date in American history is brought to you by

_____

Complete the chart below.

In the early 1800s, waterwheels were a much more important power source for industry than steam. By the late 1800s, there were four steam engines for every waterwheel. Steam powered the industrial boom of the late 1800s.

STEAM ENGINES

How They Were Important to Industrialization	
What They Were Used For	
Why They Needed Coal	

This important date in American history is brought to you by

_____

★ Beginning in 1880 ★

American Industry Booms

Study the illustration below. Then, write a caption for it that tells about the industrial boom of the late 1800s. Your caption should tell why industry boomed, what some important industries were, and how this rapid industrial growth affected the United States.

_____

_____

_____

_____

_____

This important date in American history is brought to you by

_____

★ Andrew Carnegie ★

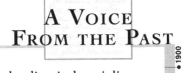

Andrew Carnegie (1835–1919) was one of the leading industrialists and wealthiest men of his time. He immigrated with his family from Scotland when he was 12 years old. As a young man, Carnegie worked at a cotton mill and as a telegraph operator. Later in life, he made a fortune selling steel through his Carnegie Steel Company.

Read the passage written by Carnegie below. Then, answer the questions.

"The eighth wonder of the world is this: two pounds of iron-stone purchased on the shores of lake Superior and transported to Pittsburgh; two pounds of coal mined in Connellsville and manufactured into coke and brought to Pittsburgh; one-half pound of limestone mined east of the Alleghenies and brought to Pittsburgh; a little manganese ore mined in Virginia and brought to Pittsburgh. And these four and one-half pounds of material manufactured into one pound of solid steel and sold for one cent. That's all that need be said about the steel business."

Why do you think Carnegie called steel a "wonder of the world"? _____

_____

_____

Carnegie only mentions the raw materials needed to make steel and does not mention the thousands of workers who mined, transported, and turned the materials into steel. Why do you think Carnegie did this? _____

_____

What did Carnegie mean when he stated, "That's all that need be said about the steel business"? _____

_____

_____

This important person in American history is brought to you by

_____

★1876★ The Telephone

Complete the information below.

THE TELEPHONE

Invented By: _____

First Words Spoken on a Telephone: _____

_____

_____

_____

When and Where the First Telephone
Exchange Opened:

_____

_____

_____

_____

Why the Telephone Is Important: _____

_____

_____

_____

_____

_____

This important date in American history is brought to you by

_____

Answer the questions below.

THE MAN

When did he live? _____

What was his home state? _____

What words would you use to describe him? _____

_____

HIS WORK

What are some things Edison invented or significantly improved? _____

_____

_____

_____

_____

When did Edison invent the lightbulb? _____

Where did Edison do most of his work? _____

HIS THOUGHTS

What do you think Edison meant by each statement below?

"There is no substitute for hard work." _____

_____

"Genius is one percent inspiration and ninety-nine percent perspiration." _____

_____

This important person in American history is brought to you by

_____

Complete the chart below.

Different parts of the modern bicycle were developed by many inventors, in many places, over many years. By the early 1890s, the modern bicycle had emerged. This time period is often called the "Golden Age" of bicycles. By 1900, more than ten million Americans—about one out of seven—rode bikes. In the early 1900s, however, the number of bicycle riders decreased dramatically.

THE BICYCLE

Advantages	
Disadvantages	
Impact on American Roads	
Why Numbers Declined in Early 1900s	

This important date in American history is brought to you by

_____

Complete the chart below.

Inventors in the United States and Europe had been working with steam-powered vehicles since the late 1700s. In the 1880s, the gasoline engine was developed and fitted to simple vehicles. In 1895, the Duryea brothers of Massachusetts set up the first American company to build gasoline-powered automobiles. Mass production of gasoline automobiles began in the United States in 1901. The picture shows the most popular automobile of the early 1900s—the Ford Model T.

THE AUTOMOBILE

Why Americans Wanted Automobiles	
Early American Auto Companies	
Major Effects of the Automobile	

This important date in American history is brought to you by

_____

★ **1903** ★ The Airplane

Answer the questions below.

Who invented the airplane? _____

_____

What type of work did they do? _____

_____

Where was their first flight? _____

_____

How far and how long was the first flight? _____

_____

What were airplanes used for in the early 1900s? _____

_____

_____

This important date in American history is brought to you by

_____

Label the following items on the map below: states in 1900, territories held by the United States in 1900, several major cities, and major bodies of water.

Fill in the missing information below. Record the total population, and shade the circle graph to illustrate the rural/urban distribution.

THE UNITED STATES IN 1900

Total Population: _____

Rural/Urban Distribution: _____

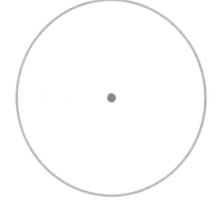

This important date in American history is brought to you by

_____

Activate the Time Machine to learn about American roads in the late 1800s and early 1900s. In the left-hand circle, write facts about American roads during that time. In the right-hand circle, write facts about American roads today. In the space where the circles overlap, write facts about American roads that both time periods have in common.

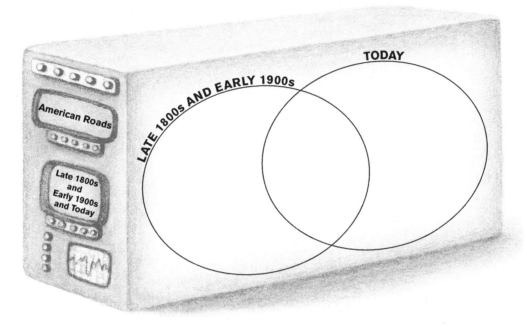

In the late 1800s, many of America's roads had gone into decline. There had been little reason to make and maintain roads since most of the nation's freight was carried by railroad.

Virtually all of the rural roads in the country — and many urban roads — were little more than narrow dirt paths. They were suitable for horses and wagons but not for the new technologies of bicycles and automobiles.

That began to change in the 1880s. Surprisingly, the first advocates of better roads were not automobile owners; they were bicyclists! Bicycle owners lobbied the government hard to provide more roads and to improve existing roads.

Automobile owners soon joined the campaign. In 1900, there were only about 8,000 automobiles in the country. Twenty years later, there were more than eight million — an increase of more than a thousand times.

The government responded with a road-building frenzy. In 1904, there were only about 100 miles of paved rural roads; most of the rural roads were dirt. By 1920, there were 35,000 miles of paved country roads.

This important trip into American history is brought to you by

_____

★ Wright Brothers
National Memorial ★

The Wright Brothers National Memorial now stands where Orville and Wilbur Wright first flew their airplane. What is it like to visit there? Conduct research to find out.

Use the Internet or any other resources your teacher suggests. Read the articles and study the illustrations. When you have gathered enough information, make a postcard.

On the front of the postcard, draw a picture or attach a picture from a magazine or the Internet that gives some information about the Wright Brothers National Memorial. On the back of the postcard, write a caption that explains the picture. Then, write a note to a friend that tells about things to do and see at the site.

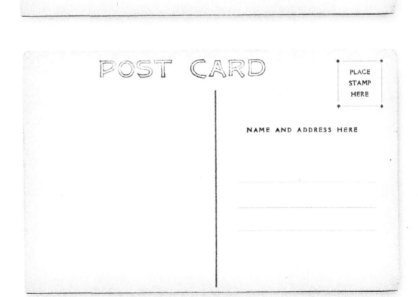

POST CARD

PLACE STAMP HERE

NAME AND ADDRESS HERE

This important place in American history is brought to you by

UNIT 2   Big Business and Social Reform

1870–1910

UNIT OVERVIEW

The emergence of big businesses—and their abuses that inspired the Progressive Movement—are hallmarks of this period of American history.

This unit focuses on these developments. Units 1 and 3 address other historical developments of this time period.

Activity Sheet 2-A provides a unit overview. Activity Sheets 2-B through 2-E highlight the major developments in business during this period, focusing on business organization, robber barons, and the corruption that went hand in hand with these businessmen and their practices.

The spotlight then shifts to the workers of this time period, most of whom were immigrants. Activity Sheet 2-F graphically depicts the wave of immigration to the United States, and Activity Sheet 2-G focuses on the Statue of Liberty, which greeted so many of the immigrants when they arrived. Activity Sheet 2-H analyzes the causes and effects of urbanization, which was largely a result of the growing industries and businesses of the period and which contributed to the difficult lives of workers. Activity Sheet 2-I focuses on poor working conditions.

The final part of the unit addresses attempts at reform. Activity Sheet 2-J covers the labor movement, and Activity Sheet 2-K addresses federal attempts at business regulation. The Progressive Movement—a broad term that included labor, social, and government action—is the subject of Activity Sheet 2-L. Jane Addams, a leading voice for social reform, is quoted extensively on Activity Sheet 2-M. The students research the "muckrakers" on Activity Sheet 2-N.

The Time Machine, Activity Sheet 2-O, compares public transportation today to public transportation during the late nineteenth century. A Postcard From the Past, Activity Sheet 2-P, is about the Statue of Liberty and Ellis Island National Monuments.

FOCUS ACTIVITIES

To focus the students' attention on this period of American history, consider the following activities:

What's in a Name?

Ask the students what they associate with the names Rockefeller and Carnegie (wealth). Tell the students that during this time period, the "Gilded Age," some people were extremely rich. Give a few examples of things people spent excessive amounts of money on, like elaborate mansions. Explain that the students are going to learn how such fortunes were made and how these extremely rich people affected the course of U.S. history.

Lady Liberty

Share with the students this excerpt from Emma Lazarus's famous poem (inscribed on the pedestal of the Statue of Liberty): "Give me your tired, your poor,/Your huddled masses yearning to breathe free,/The wretched refuse of your teeming shore./Send these, the homeless, tempest-tost to me,/I lift my lamp beside the golden door!" Help the students interpret this excerpt within the context of immigration to the United States.

Regulation and Deregulation

Hold a classroom debate on the degree to which government should regulate business. Explain how modern government regulation of business arose from the abuses and corruption of businesses during this period of American history.

CONSTRUCTING THE TIMELINE

This unit consists of 16 activity sheets that focus on significant events, people, and places related to big business and social reform during the late nineteenth and early twentieth centuries. Each activity sheet is designed to, once completed, become part of a posted classroom timeline of the period covered in the unit.

The Introduction (pages VII–XIII) provides a detailed explanation of how to use the activity sheets in the classroom and suggests various ways to construct the timeline using the completed activity sheets.

You can construct the timeline any way you see fit. Use the Timeline Components (pages XVIII–XXV) to connect the activity sheets. Below are two possible timelines, constructed from the activity sheets in this unit and the Timeline Components.

Option 1: Basic Timeline

Construct this timeline to identify only the essential elements of the period.

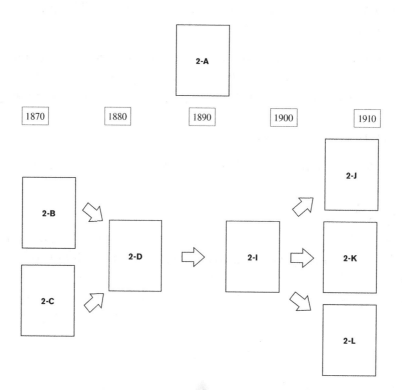

Option 2: Complete Timeline

Construct this timeline to identify the essential elements of the period, examine them in greater detail, and extend student learning.

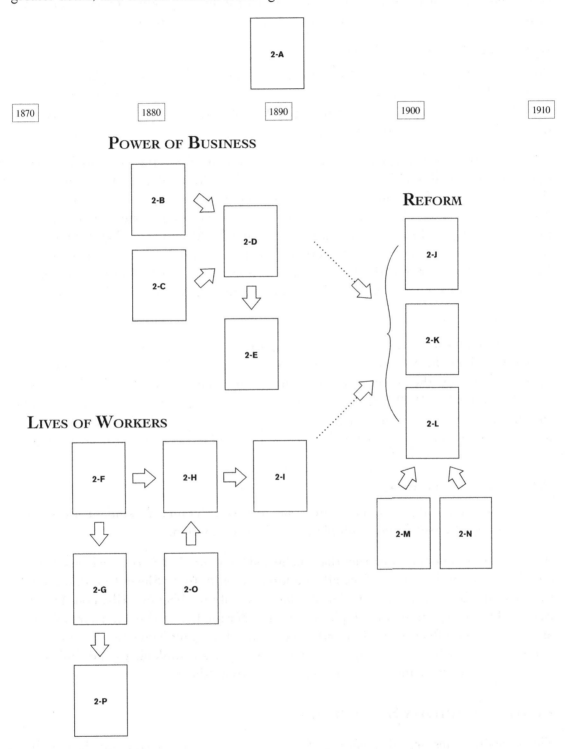

CRITICAL THINKING SKILLS

The activity sheets in this unit address various critical thinking skills. In addition, the constructed timeline emphasizes the essential critical thinking skills of identifying main ideas and details, sequencing events, and relating causes and effects.

Identifying Main Ideas and Details

Point out that Activity Sheet 2-A outlines the main ideas of the unit. Explain that the topics of the other activity sheets in the unit reflect the main ideas of the historical period the students are studying. Further explain that some activity sheets focus on the details related to specific topics.

As you and the students construct the timeline, show them that the first subheading is a main idea while Activity Sheets 2-B through 2-E focus on details. Point out the similar relationship between the second subheading and Activity Sheets 2-F through 2-I and Activity Sheets 2-O and 2-P, as well as the similar relationship between the third subheading and Activity Sheets 2-J through 2-N. Also explain that Activity Sheet 2-L covers a main idea while Activity Sheets 2-M and 2-N focus on details. Have the students annotate the Timeline Arrows appropriately. Challenge the students to find similar relationships or create them by rearranging the activity sheets.

Sequencing Events

Point out that the activity sheets that make up the timeline are sequential. Show the students how the Timeline Dates provide a concrete reference for when events happened and how they relate to other events. (For example, working conditions were poor during the late 1800s before the Progressive Movement in the early 1900s.) Make sure the students see that the Timeline Arrows indicate a chronological flow from left to right. Also, remind the students that this unit's timeline has three basic layers that are separated by subheadings.

Relating Causes and Effects

Review the relationship between a cause and an effect. Remind the students that there can be multiple causes and/or multiple effects in any situation.

As you and the students construct the timeline, show them that Activity Sheets 2-B and 2-C focus on the causes of the effect addressed on Activity Sheet 2-D. Point out that Activity Sheets 2-F and 2-H discuss the causes of the effect described on Activity Sheet 2-I. Also explain that the topics covered under the first and second subheadings are causes of the effects discussed under the third subheading. Have the students annotate the Timeline Arrows appropriately. Challenge the students to find similar relationships or create them by rearranging the activity sheets.

INDIVIDUAL ACTIVITY SHEET NOTES

The following notes provide a variety of tips on how to guide the students through the completion and extension of each activity sheet.

2-A. Big Business and Social Reform

This activity is most appropriate for the students to complete with partners, in small groups, or as a whole class. For example, you might want to complete the questions with the whole class at the beginning of the unit and then have the students answer the questions at the end of the unit. Encourage the students to think of additional questions related to the topic.

2-B. Corporations, Trusts, and Monopolies

Emphasize that the organization of large businesses was based on the desire to enhance the wealth and power of the relatively few people who controlled the businesses. Explain that the power these people had could be compared to powerful government officials. Tell the students that the Supreme Court ruled that, according to the law, corporations were "persons deserving the law's due process."

2-C. Robber Barons

Engage the students in a discussion about what motivated these people (for example, wealth, power, or concern for their fellow Americans). Ask the students if they think that such economic success carries with it any responsibilities.

2-D. Business Corruption

Make sure the students understand that most of the current laws designed to uncover and punish such corrupt practices did not exist during the late nineteenth and early twentieth centuries. In fact, it was the corruption of this period that led, directly and indirectly, to many of the laws that are in force today.

2-E. Biography: John D. Rockefeller

If appropriate, share and discuss all or part of the following statement made by Rockefeller: "God gave me my money. I believe the power to make money is a gift from God.... I believe it is my duty to make money and still more money and to use the money I make for the good of my fellow man according to the dictates of my conscience."

2-F. A Wave of Immigrants

Ask the students why the United States is often called "a nation of immigrants." Make sure the students understand the "push" and "pull" of immigration to the United States. Immigrants were "pushed" out of their homelands by social, economic, and political situations and "pulled" to the United States by the hope of making a better life.

2-G. The Statue of Liberty

Invite a student who has visited the Statue of Liberty to share his or her experience with the class. Have another student read Emma Lazarus's poem "The New Colossus" to the class.

2-H. Urbanization

Challenge the students to explain the relationship among industrialization, immigration, and urbanization during this period of American history.

2-I. Working Conditions

Tell the students that it is difficult to overstate the abuse of working people during this time. Child labor was common, as were a lack of safety procedures and devices, six- and seven-day work weeks, ten- and twelve-hour workdays, and abusively low wages.

2-J. The Labor Movement

Ask the students to share what they know about common working conditions today. Discuss that most jobs include five-day, forty-hour work weeks; safety rules; and vacation and sick leave. Point out that there was a time when none of these existed but that things changed because of the labor movement, which was born during this period of American history.

2-K. Government Regulation of Big Business

Make sure the students understand that the Clayton Antitrust Act was passed to strengthen the Sherman Antitrust Act. The Clayton Antitrust Act addressed specific things businesses could not do. The year it was passed, 1914, also saw the birth of the Federal Trade Commission and marked the government's commitment to the regulation of business.

2-L. The Progressive Movement

Have the students explain why the term "progressive" is appropriate as the name of this movement. Discuss what people were "progressing toward." Ask the students how the term and the movement are still facets of American life today.

2-M. A Voice From the Past: Jane Addams

Ask the students to draw comparisons between the nature and purposes of Hull House and similar private and public institutions today.

2-N. Muckrakers

Explain that the application of the term "muckrakers" to crusading journalists was originally used, by Theodore Roosevelt, as something of an insult. He said, "The men with the muckrakes are often indispensable to the well-being of society, but only if they know when to stop raking the muck, and to look upward to the celestial crown above them." (It was an allusion to the man with the muckrake in *Pilgrim's Progress*, by John Bunyan.)

2-O. Time Machine: Public Transportation

Help the students identify the main points of the essay, which should be written in the left-hand circle of the Venn diagram.

2-P. A Postcard From the Past: The Statue of Liberty and Ellis Island National Monuments

Suggest that the students visit www.nps.gov (the web site of the National Park Service) to gather information about the Statue of Liberty and Ellis Island National Monuments.

Big Business and Social Reform

In the box below, draw a picture or attach a picture from a magazine or the Internet that represents big business or social reform during this period of American history. The picture can be of anything you think is appropriate.

Ask questions about big business or social reform during this period of American history. Then, answer them.

Question: WHO_____?

Answer:_____

Question: WHAT_____?

Answer:_____

Question: WHERE _____?

Answer:_____

Question: WHEN _____?

Answer:_____

Question: WHY_____?

Answer:_____

Question: HOW_____?

Answer:_____

This important date in American history is brought to you by

_____

★ 1870s ★ Corporations, Trusts, and Monopolies

Complete the diagram below by writing a definition for each term.

Corporation	
Trust	
Monopoly	

This important date in American history is brought to you by

_____

1800 1810 1820 1830 1840 1850 1860 1870 1880 1890 1900

Answer the questions below.

What was a robber baron? _____

Why were some people called robber barons? _____

_____

How did they make their fortunes? _____

_____

Use the Internet or any other resources your teacher suggests to identify the person in each picture below.

| Jay Gould | Cornelius Vanderbilt | Andrew Carnegie | J.P. Morgan | John D. Rockefeller |

a. _____

d. _____

c. _____

b. _____

e. _____

These important people in American history are brought to you by

_____

Write a newspaper article about corruption in big business during the late 1800s. Your article can be a news article or an editorial.

CORRUPTION IN BIG BUSINESS!

_____

_____

_____

_____

_____

_____

_____

_____

_____

_____

_____

This important date in American history is brought to you by

_____

Answer the questions below.

THE MAN

When did he live? _____

Where was he born? _____

What words would you use to describe him? _____

_____

_____

HIS BUSINESS

What natural resource was Rockefeller most concerned with? _____

What trust did he create in 1882? _____

What made this company so successful? _____

_____

_____

What happened to this company? _____

_____

_____

_____

This important person in American history is brought to you by

_____

★Late 1800s and Early 1900s★

A Wave of Immigrants

Use the data in the chart below to make a bar graph in the box below. Give the graph an appropriate title.

Decade	Number of Immigrants Admitted (in millions)
1861–1870	2.32
1871–1880	2.81
1881–1890	5.25
1891–1900	3.69
1901–1910	8.8
1911–1920	5.74
1921–1930	4.11

These important dates in American history are brought to you by

Answer the questions below.

Where is the Statue of Liberty? _____

_____

Who designed it? _____

_____

Who gave the statue to the United States?

_____

What does the Statue of Liberty represent?

_____

Why was this statue important to so
many immigrants?

_____

_____

_____

What are some interesting facts about the
Statue of Liberty?

_____

_____

_____

_____

_____

This important date in American history is brought to you by

_____

★ Late 1800s ★ Urbanization

Complete the chart below.

URBANIZATION

Definition	
Causes	
Effects	

These important facts in American history are brought to you by

_____

Study the illustration below. Then, write a caption for it that tells about working conditions in factories during the late 1800s. Your caption should tell what the conditions were like and why they were so bad.

_____

_____

_____

_____

_____

_____

This important date in American history is brought to you by

_____

★ Late 1800s ★ The Labor Movement

Complete the chart below.

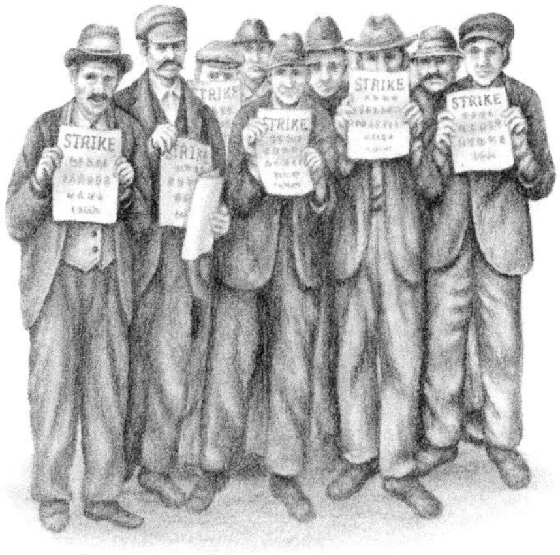

The Labor Movement

What It Was	
Its Goals	
Important Labor Leaders	
Major Labor Organizations	
Ways People Tried to Accomplish the Goals of the Labor Movement	
Significant Accomplishments	

This important date in American history is brought to you by

____

Government Regulation
of Big Business

Complete the diagram below. Write important facts about each law in the appropriate
circle. In the spaces where the circles overlap, write facts about what the laws had in
common. Make sure to explain why these laws were necessary.

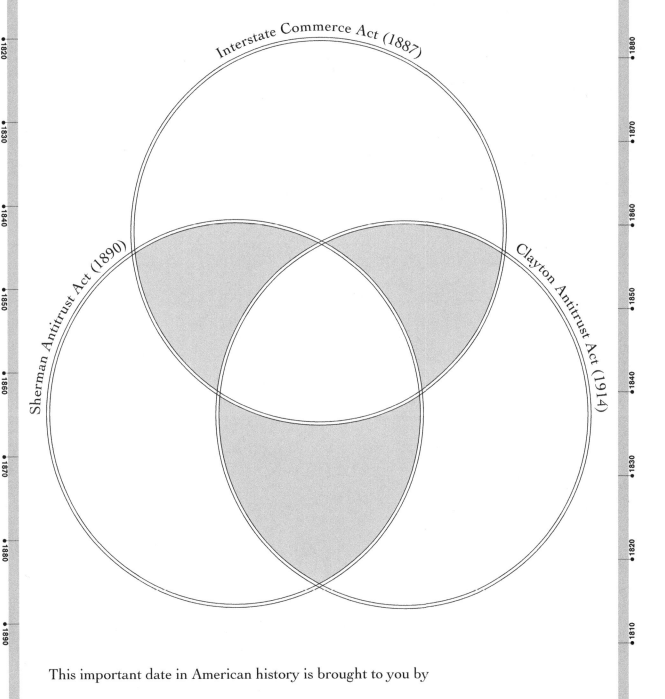

Interstate Commerce Act (1887)

Sherman Antitrust Act (1890)

Clayton Antitrust Act (1914)

This important date in American history is brought to you by

_____

★ Late 1800s and Early 1900s ★

The Progressive Movement

Complete the chart below.

THE PROGRESSIVE MOVEMENT

What It Was	
Its Goals	
The Meaning of the Movement's Name	
Important Leaders	
Major Organizations	
Ways People Tried to Accomplish the Goals of the Progressive Movement	
Significant Accomplishments	

These important facts in American history are brought to you by

_____

Timeline markings (left side, top to bottom): 1800, 1810, 1820, 1830, 1840, 1850, 1860, 1870, 1880, 1890, 1900

Timeline markings (right side, top to bottom): 1900, 1890, 1880, 1870, 1860, 1850, 1840, 1830, 1820, 1810, 1800

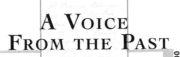

In 1889, Jane Addams and Ellen Gates Starr established Hull House in a poor neighborhood in Chicago. Hull House was a "settlement house"—a place for homeless people to live and receive vital healthcare, education, and other social services. Hull House became the most famous settlement house in the country, and Jane Addams became the most important social reformer of her time.

Read what Addams wrote below. Then, answer the questions.

"The policy of the public authorities of never taking an initiative, and always waiting to be urged to do their duty, is obviously fatal in a neighborhood where there is little initiative among the citizens.…The streets are inexpressibly dirty, the number of schools inadequate, sanitary legislation unenforced, the street lighting bad, the paving miserable and altogether lacking in the alleys and smaller streets, and the stables foul beyond description. Hundreds of houses are unconnected with the street sewer. The older and richer inhabitants seem anxious to move away as rapidly as they can afford it.…

In those early days we were often asked why we had come to live [there] when we could afford to live somewhere else.…In time it came to seem natural to all of us that [we] should be there. If it is natural to feed the hungry and care for the sick, it is certainly natural to give pleasure to the young, comfort to the aged, and to minister to the deep-seated craving for social intercourse that all men feel. Whoever does it is rewarded by something…spontaneous and vital.…

Perhaps even in those first days we made a beginning toward that object which was afterwards stated in our charter: To provide a center for a higher civic and social life; to institute and maintain educational and philanthropic enterprises; and to investigate and improve the conditions in the industrial districts of Chicago."

What was the goal of Hull House?

_____

_____

Why did Addams do what she did?

_____

_____

This important person in American history is brought to you by

_____

★ Late 1800s and Early 1900s ★

Muckrakers

JACOB RIIS

Famous Work:

Date of Publication:

What It Exposed:

UPTON SINCLAIR

Famous Work:

Date of Publication:

What It Exposed:

LINCOLN STEFFENS

Famous Work:

Date of Publication:

What It Exposed:

IDA M. TARBELL

Famous Work:

Date of Publication:

What It Exposed:

These important people in American history are brought to you by

_____

Activate the Time Machine to learn about public transportation in the 1890s. In the left-hand circle, write facts about public transportation during that time. In the right-hand circle, write facts about public transportation today. In the space where the circles overlap, write facts about public transportation that both time periods have in common.

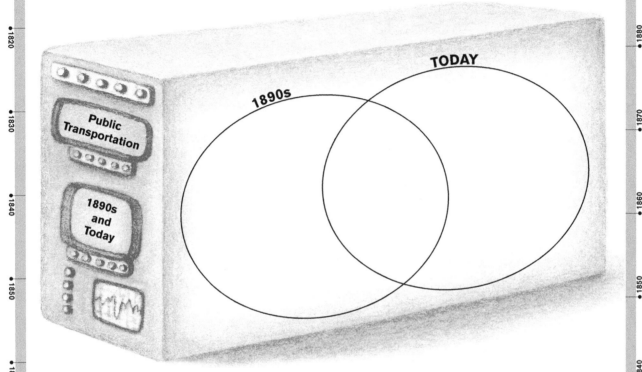

In the 1890s, using public transportation meant taking the trolley. The trolley looked like a railroad car. It had windows all the way around and a glass compartment where the driver sat. There were seats inside for the passengers.

Trolleys ran on tracks similar to railroad tracks. The trolleys were driven by electric motors. The motors received electricity from wires that were strung from poles over the tracks.

In the 1890s, hundreds of American cities had trolleys. There were more than 20,000 miles of trolley tracks in the United States. The trolleys ran on regular schedules and made regular stops. People used them to get to and from work, the store, homes of friends and relatives, and places of entertainment. The fare was typically a nickel.

This important trip into American history is brought to you by

_____

★ The Statue of Liberty and Ellis Island National Monuments ★

The Statue of Liberty is one of the most famous landmarks in the world. Nearby Ellis Island, where millions of immigrants were admitted into the United States, is also famous. Today, they are both national monuments. What is it like to visit them? Conduct research to find out.

Use the Internet or any other resources your teacher suggests. Read the articles and study the illustrations. When you have gathered enough information, make a postcard.

On the front of the postcard, draw a picture or attach a picture from a magazine or the Internet that shows the Statue of Liberty or Ellis Island. On the back of the postcard, write a caption that explains the picture. Then, write a note to a friend that tells about things to do and see at the site.

POST CARD

PLACE STAMP HERE

NAME AND ADDRESS HERE

This important place in American history is brought to you by

1867–1910

UNIT OVERVIEW

Fueled by its inventive and growing population, its industrial might, and its bold policies, the United States emerged as a global power during this period of American history.

This unit focuses on these developments. Units 1 and 2 address other historical developments during this time period.

Activity Sheet 3-A provides a unit overview. Activity Sheets 3-B and 3-E identify the last major state territorial acquisitions of the United States: the Alaska Purchase and the Hawaii Annexation. Activity Sheets 3-C and 3-D focus on the Spanish-American War and how it was affected by yellow journalism. Activity Sheet 3-F identifies the territories that the United States acquired as a result of the Spanish-American War.

Activity Sheets 3-G through 3-K focus on President Theodore Roosevelt, whose "big stick" policy was instrumental in gaining America's place on the world stage. Activity Sheet 3-G provides a biographical sketch of the man, and Activity Sheet 3-H focuses on some of his most memorable quotations. Activity Sheet 3-I discusses the Panama Canal, and Activity Sheet 3-J explains the famous Roosevelt Corollary to the Monroe Doctrine. Activity Sheet 3-K, about the Great White Fleet, is concerned with an often overlooked, yet highly symbolic, historical event. The growth of the United States as a world power, and the reasons for this development, are summarized on Activity Sheet 3-L. Activity Sheet 3-M provides a geographic and demographic snapshot of the United States in 1910.

The Time Machine, Activity Sheet 3-N, compares journalism today to journalism during the late nineteenth century. A Postcard From the Past, Activity Sheet 3-O, is about Sagamore Hill National Historic Site.

FOCUS ACTIVITIES

To focus the students' attention on this period of American history, consider the following activities:

The Superpower

Explain that, today, the United States is considered to be the one and only superpower. Discuss the reasons why. Point out that this unit takes a look at the first steps the country took to becoming such a global force.

Teddy Bears

Ask the students if they know why stuffed bears are called "teddy bears." Give the students the hint that teddy bears are named after Theodore ("Teddy") Roosevelt. Have the students conduct research to find out why. Then, discuss the appropriateness of the connection between a child's soft toy and the man who wielded the "big stick" and led the "strenuous life."

Arctic and Tropic

Invite the students to share and then compare and contrast their general impressions of Alaska (cold and rugged) and Hawaii (warm and beautiful). Point out that the students will learn how each of these remarkable places became part of the United States.

CONSTRUCTING THE TIMELINE

This unit consists of 15 activity sheets that focus on significant events, people, and places related to the emergence of America as a global power during the late nineteenth and early twentieth centuries. Each activity sheet is designed to, once completed, become part of a posted classroom timeline of the period covered in the unit.

The Introduction (pages VII–XIII) provides a detailed explanation of how to use the activity sheets in the classroom and suggests various ways to construct the timeline using the completed activity sheets.

You can construct the timeline any way you see fit. Use the Timeline Components (pages XVIII–XXV) to connect the activity sheets. Below are two possible timelines, constructed from the activity sheets in this unit and the Timeline Components.

Option 1: Basic Timeline

Construct this timeline to identify only the essential elements of the period.

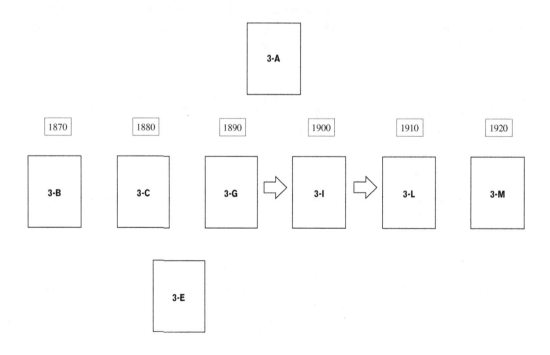

Option 2: Complete Timeline

Construct this timeline to identify the essential elements of the period, examine them in greater detail, and extend student learning.

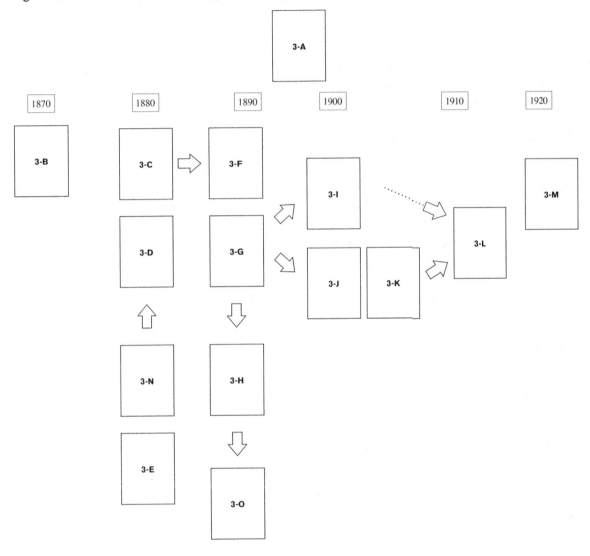

CRITICAL THINKING SKILLS

The activity sheets in this unit address various critical thinking skills. In addition, the constructed timeline emphasizes the essential critical thinking skills of identifying main ideas and details, sequencing events, and relating causes and effects.

Identifying Main Ideas and Details

Point out that Activity Sheet 3-A outlines the main ideas of the unit. Explain that the topics of the other activity sheets in the unit reflect the main ideas of the historical period the students are studying. Further explain that some activity sheets focus on the details related to specific topics.

As you and the students construct the timeline, show them that Activity Sheet 3-G forms a main idea and Activity Sheets 3-H through 3-K and Activity Sheet 3-O focus on details. Have the students annotate the Timeline Arrows appropriately. Challenge the students to find similar relationships or create them by rearranging the activity sheets.

Sequencing Events

Point out that the activity sheets that make up the timeline are sequential. Show the students how the Timeline Dates provide a concrete reference for when events happened and how they relate to other events. (For example, the Panama Canal was built in 1903 before the Great White Fleet's journey in 1907.) Make sure the students see that the Timeline Arrows indicate a chronological flow from left to right. Emphasize the sequence of events from Activity Sheet 3-C to Activity Sheet 3-L.

Relating Causes and Effects

As you and the students construct the timeline, show them that the following activity sheets form cause/effect relationships: 3-D/3-C; 3-C/3-F; 3-G/3-I, 3-J, 3-K; and 3-I, 3-J, 3-K/3-L. Have the students annotate the Timeline Arrows appropriately. Challenge the students to find similar relationships or create them by rearranging the activity sheets.

INDIVIDUAL ACTIVITY SHEET NOTES

The notes below provide a variety of tips on how to guide the students through the completion and extension of each activity sheet.

3-A. America and the World

This activity is most appropriate for the students to complete with partners, in small groups, or as a whole class. For example, you might want to complete the questions with the whole class at the beginning of the unit and then have the students answer the questions at the end of the unit. Encourage the students to think of additional questions related to the topic.

3-B. Map Study: The Alaska Purchase

Have the students consider why this purchase was called "Seward's Folly" and "Seward's Icebox." Have them calculate the cost per square mile.

3-C. The Spanish-American War

Make sure the students understand the imperial nature of the war. Point out that recent evidence seems to indicate that the explosion of the *Maine* may have been accidental.

3-D. Yellow Journalism

Emphasize the fact that yellow journalism was driven by the desire to make money. In many cases, newspaper rivalry was bitter.

3-E. Map Study: The Hawaii Annexation

Make sure the students understand the role American businessmen played in the annexation of Hawaii.

3-F. Map Study: New American Territories

Have the students conduct research to find out the current political state of these territories (e.g., which ones are still under American control, are independent countries, etc.).

3-G. Biography: Theodore Roosevelt

Make sure the students understand that Roosevelt was a great champion of conservation. Remind the students that teddy bears are named after Teddy Roosevelt.

3-H. A Voice From the Past: Theodore Roosevelt

As an alternative activity, you might choose to have the students rewrite the quotations in their own words. Guide the students into seeing how all of the quotations are still relevant today, in the students' own lives and to the country as a whole. Discuss the meaning of each line with the students. Emphasize the words, "the shot heard 'round the world," in the last line.

3-I. The Panama Canal

Have the students trace sea routes on the map with and without using the canal. This will give the students a better understanding of how much travel distance the canal saved then and still saves today. Tell the students about America's creation of the country of Panama (from Colombian territory) to facilitate the building of the canal.

3-J. The Roosevelt Corollary

Ask the students to find out whether the Roosevelt Corollary is still part of America's foreign policy. Have them cite recent developments to support their answers.

3-K. The Great White Fleet

Make sure the students understand that the purpose of the Great White Fleet was to demonstrate American power, especially to Japan. The U.S. Navy realized that it was highly dependent on foreign sources of supplies during long, distant cruises, so it worked to establish distant bases.

3-L. A World Power

Have the students evaluate the merit of this development in American—and world—history. Ask the students the following questions: Should the United States have become a world power? What happened as a result? Was this a plan, an accident of history, or both? What are the advantages and disadvantages of having such a large impact on the world?

3-M. Map Study: The United States in 1910

Emphasize the growing population of the United States and its increasing urbanization.

3-N. The Time Machine: Journalism

Help the students identify the main points of the essay, which should be written in the left-hand circle of the Venn diagram.

3-O. A Postcard From the Past: Sagamore Hill National Historic Site

Suggest that the students visit www.nps.gov (the web site of the National Park Service) to gather information about Sagamore Hill National Historic Site.

America and the World

In the box below, draw a picture or attach a picture from a magazine or the Internet that represents America's growing involvement in world affairs during this period of American history. The picture can be of anything you think is appropriate.

Ask questions about America's growing involvement in world affairs during this period of American history. Then, answer them.

Question: WHO_____?

Answer:_____

Question: WHAT_____?

Answer:_____

Question: WHERE _____?

Answer:_____

Question: WHEN _____?

Answer:_____

Question: WHY_____?

Answer:_____

Question: HOW_____?

Answer:_____

This important date in American history is brought to you by

_____

Shade and label the United States in 1867 on the map below. Shade and label the Alaska Purchase. Then, complete the chart.

THE ALASKA PURCHASE

Area of Territory	
From Whom It Was Acquired	
How It Was Acquired	
Current State(s) in Territory	

This important date in American history is brought to you by

_____

Complete the diagram below.

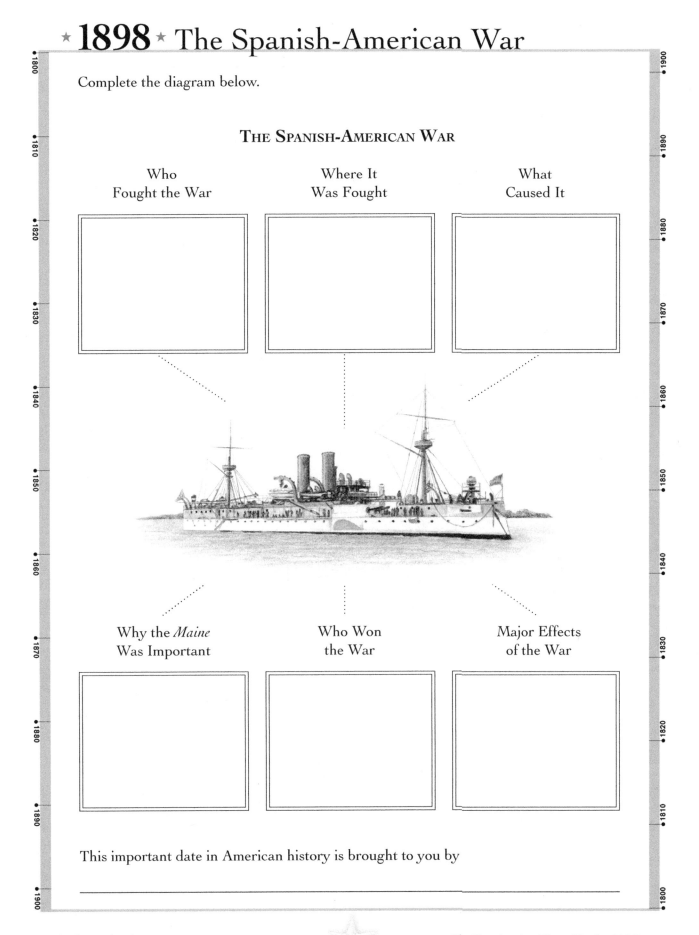

THE SPANISH-AMERICAN WAR

Who
Fought the War

Where It
Was Fought

What
Caused It

Why the *Maine*
Was Important

Who Won
the War

Major Effects
of the War

This important date in American history is brought to you by

_____

Yellow Journalism

Complete the chart below.

YELLOW JOURNALISM!

Definition	
Effects	
Roles Played by William Randolph Hearst and Joseph Pulitzer	

These important facts in American history are brought to you by

_____

Shade and label the United States in 1898. Then, shade and label the Hawaii Annexation and complete the chart.

THE HAWAII ANNEXATION

Area of Territory	
From Whom It Was Acquired	
How It Was Acquired	
Current State(s) in Territory	

This important date in American history is brought to you by

_____

Timeline markings (left): 1800, 1810, 1820, 1830, 1840, 1850, 1860, 1870, 1880, 1890, 1900

Timeline markings (right): 1900, 1890, 1880, 1870, 1860, 1850, 1840, 1830, 1820, 1810, 1800

Complete the chart below. Then, shade and label the United States and its territories on the map.

U.S. Territories Gained
Because of the Spanish-American War

Name of Territory	Location

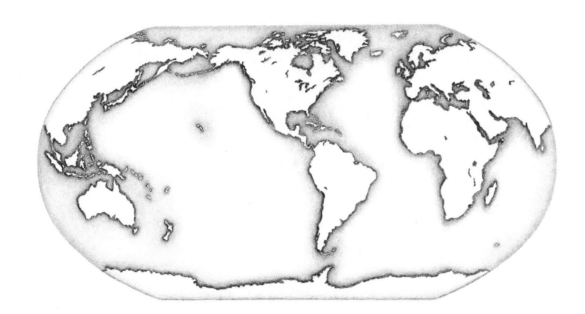

This important date in American history is brought to you by

_____

1800 1810 1820 1830 1840 1850 1860 1870 1880 1890 1900

1900 1890 1880 1870 1860 1850 1840 1830 1820 1810 1800

Answer the questions below.

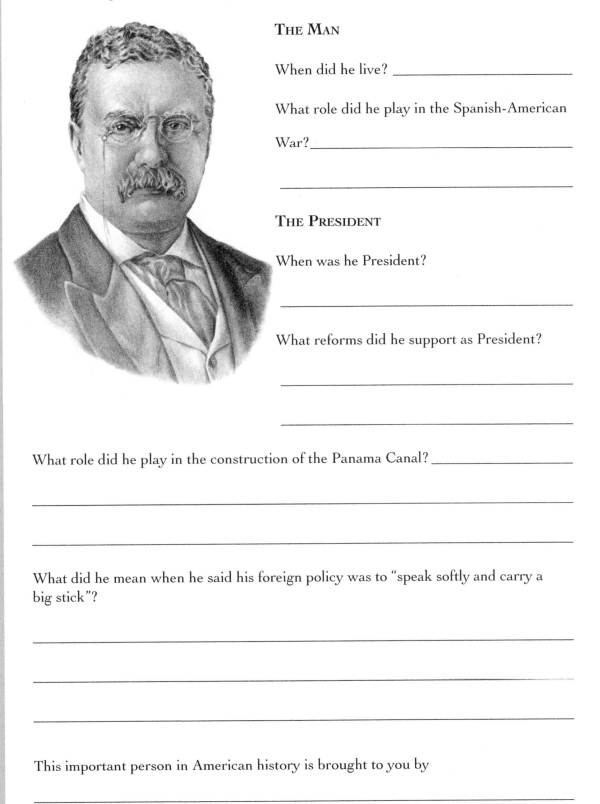

THE MAN

When did he live? _____

What role did he play in the Spanish-American

War? _____

_____

THE PRESIDENT

When was he President?

_____

What reforms did he support as President?

_____

_____

What role did he play in the construction of the Panama Canal? _____

_____

_____

What did he mean when he said his foreign policy was to "speak softly and carry a big stick"?

_____

_____

_____

This important person in American history is brought to you by

_____

Theodore Roosevelt was one of the most interesting people in American history. Weak as a boy, he built himself up physically by living what he called the "strenuous life"— hiking, swimming, boxing, and participating in other strenuous activities. He was a man of great action but also a man of powerful words. Some of his most memorable statements are recorded below. Read and think about each one. Then, explain what it means.

"Far better it is to dare mighty things, to win glorious triumphs, even though checkered by failure, than to take rank with those poor spirits who neither enjoy much nor suffer much, because they live in the gray twilight that knows not victory nor defeat." (1899)

_____

_____

_____

_____

"There is a homely adage which runs, 'Speak softly and carry a big stick; you will go far.' If the American nation will speak softly and yet build and keep at a pitch of the highest training a thoroughly efficient Navy, the Monroe Doctrine will go far." (1901)

_____

_____

_____

_____

"To waste, to destroy, our natural resources, to skin and exhaust the land instead of using it so as to increase its usefulness, will result in undermining in the days of our children the very prosperity which we ought by right to hand down to them...." (1907)

_____

_____

_____

_____

This important person in American history is brought to you by

_____

★ 1903 ★ The Panama Canal

Label the Panama Canal on the map below. Then, complete the chart.

THE PANAMA CANAL

Bodies of Water It Connects	
Why It Was Built	
Built By	
Length	
Approximate Distance Saved on a Ship's Voyage Between the East and West Coasts of the United States	

This important date in American history is brought to you by

Complete each paragraph below. Then, answer the questions.

THE MONROE DOCTRINE was put forth by President James Monroe in 1823. It stated:

_____

_____

THE ROOSEVELT COROLLARY to the Monroe Doctrine was put forth by President Theodore Roosevelt in 1904. It stated:

_____

_____

What is a "doctrine"? _____

_____

Why was Roosevelt's policy called a "Corollary to the Monroe Doctrine"? _____

_____

This important date in American history is brought to you by

_____

★ 1907 ★ The Great White Fleet

Study the illustration below. Then, write a caption for it that tells about the Great White Fleet. Your caption should tell what the Great White Fleet was, where it went, who ordered it on its journey, and what its purpose was.

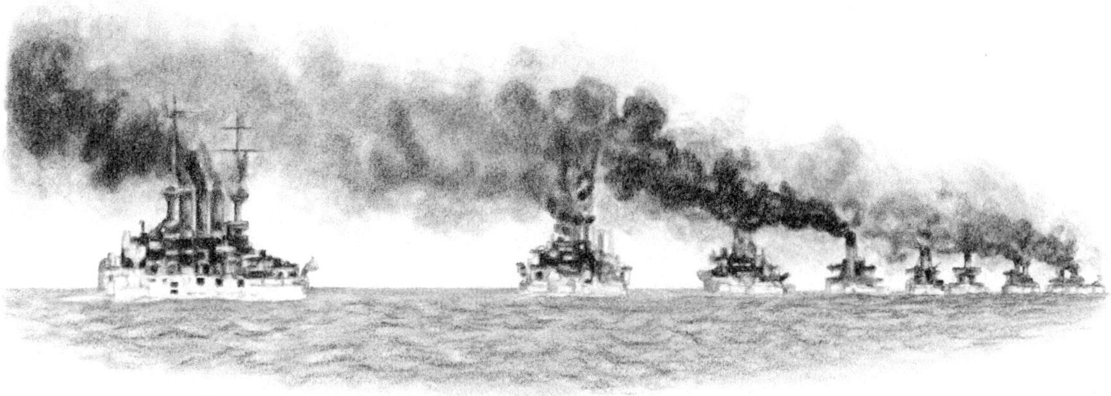

This important date in American history is brought to you by

★ Early 1900s ★ A World Power

Complete the diagram below by identifying at least five factors that led to the United States becoming a world power.

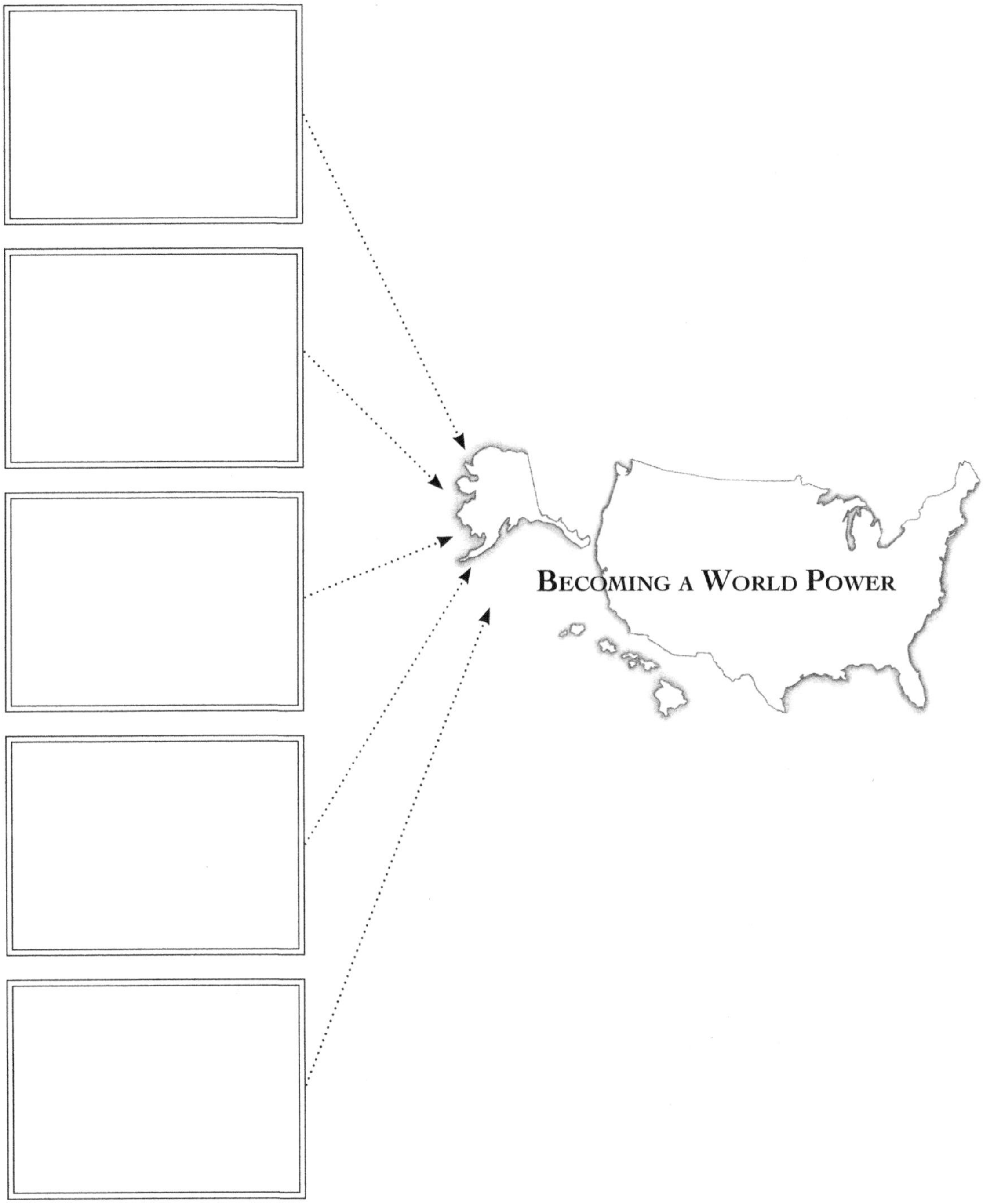

BECOMING A WORLD POWER

This important date in American history is brought to you by

_____

60

Label the following items on the map below: states in 1910, territories held by the United States in 1910, several major cities, and bodies of water.

Fill in the missing information below. Record the total population, and shade the circle graph to illustrate the rural/urban distribution.

THE UNITED STATES IN 1910

Total Population: _____

Rural/Urban Distribution: _____

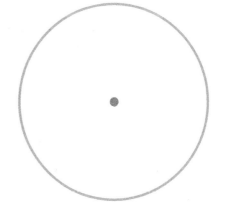

This important date in American history is brought to you by

_____

Activate the Time Machine to learn about journalism during the late 1890s. In the left-hand circle, write facts about journalism during that time. In the right-hand circle, write facts about journalism today. In the space where the circles overlap, write facts about journalism that both time periods have in common.

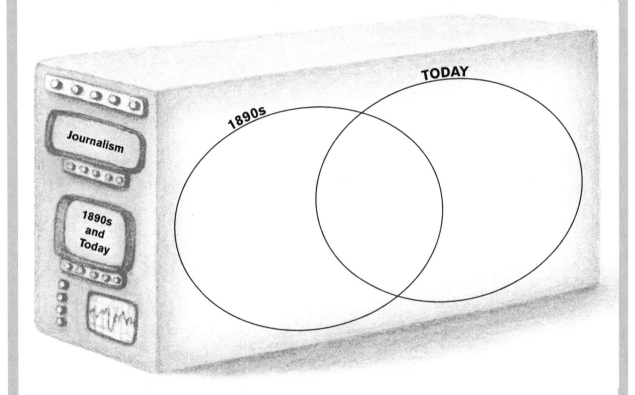

In the history of journalism, the 1890s are sometimes referred to as "the age of sensationalism." This is because newspapers ran sensational stories in order to attract readers.

Typical stories included graphic depictions of crimes, accidents, and natural disasters. Stories that reported scandals among prominent citizens were also favored by readers.

Inaccurate and exaggerated stories were commonplace. Many so-called news stories included complete lies. Such reporting is called "yellow journalism."

This was largely the result of rivalry among newspapers. Large cities had at least two or more newspapers. Each newspaper tried to outdo the others with thrilling stories that would lure readers away from its competitors.

This important trip into American history is brought to you by

_____

⋆ Sagamore Hill National Historic Site ⋆

Sagamore Hill was Theodore Roosevelt's home in New York. It was known as the "Summer White House" during his presidency. Today, Sagamore Hill is preserved as a National Historic Site. What is it like to visit there? Conduct research to find out.

Use the Internet or any other resources your teacher suggests. Read the articles, and study the illustrations. When you have gathered enough information, make a postcard.

On the front of the postcard, draw a picture or attach a picture from a magazine or the Internet that gives some information about Sagamore Hill. On the back of the postcard, write a caption that explains the picture. Then, write a note to a friend that tells about things to do and see at the site.

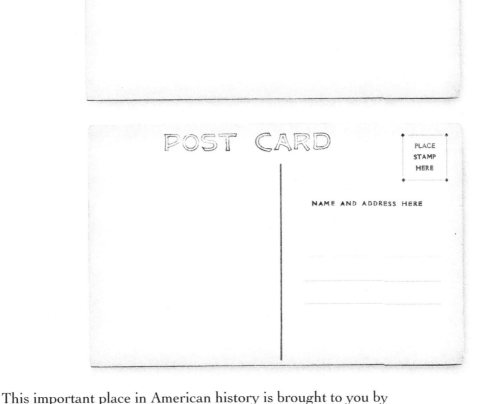

POST CARD

PLACE STAMP HERE

NAME AND ADDRESS HERE

This important place in American history is brought to you by

_____

UNIT 4 World War I

1910–1920

UNIT OVERVIEW

World War I—or the Great War, as it was known at the time—was the worst conflict the world had ever seen. This war of attrition was noted for trench-warfare bloodbaths and the clash between old tactics and new technologies. In many ways, the war marked the emergence of modern warfare and made clear the importance of the home front and industrial production to winning such a war.

Activity Sheet 4-A provides a unit overview. Activity Sheets 4-B and 4-C focus on the causes of the war in Europe. Activity Sheets 4-D through 4-F provide an overview of the war itself, with Activity Sheet 4-E marking the entry of the United States into the ongoing war. Activity Sheets 4-G and 4-H examine the types of warfare and weapons used. Activity Sheet 4-I addresses the importance of the home front. Activity Sheets 4-J through 4-L are about the outcome and aftermath of the war. Activity Sheet 4-M provides a biography of the greatest American hero of World War I, Alvin York.

The Time Machine, Activity Sheet 4-N, compares popular songs today to popular songs in the World War I era. A Postcard From the Past, Activity Sheet 4-O, is about the Liberty Memorial.

FOCUS ACTIVITIES

To focus the students' attention on this period of American history, consider the following activities:

The Great War

Tell the students that World War I was called the Great War when it was being fought and was only referred to as World War I about 15 years later. Challenge the students to explain why.

Watch a Movie

As a class, watch a movie about World War I. *Sergeant York* (1941), which stars Gary Cooper, is an excellent portrayal of the life of Alvin York. *The Lost Battalion* (2001), which stars Rick Schroder, graphically depicts the horrors of World War I combat.

The Home Front

Have the students identify some ways that civilians in the United States have contributed to the effort during times of war. Point out that the term "home front" was coined during World War I, and challenge the students to explain why this is so.

CONSTRUCTING THE TIMELINE

This unit consists of 15 activity sheets that focus on significant events, people, and places related to the World War I era. Each activity sheet is designed to, once completed, become part of a posted classroom timeline of the period covered in the unit.

The Introduction (pages VII–XIII) provides a detailed explanation of how to use the activity sheets in the classroom and suggests various ways to construct the timeline using the completed activity sheets.

You can construct the timeline any way you see fit. Use the Timeline Components (pages XVIII–XXV) to connect the activity sheets. Below are two possible timelines, constructed from the activity sheets in this unit and the Timeline Components.

Option 1: Basic Timeline

Construct this timeline to identify only the essential elements of the period.

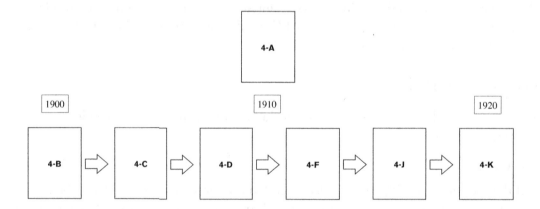

Option 2: Complete Timeline

Construct this timeline to identify the essential elements of the period, examine them in greater detail, and extend student learning.

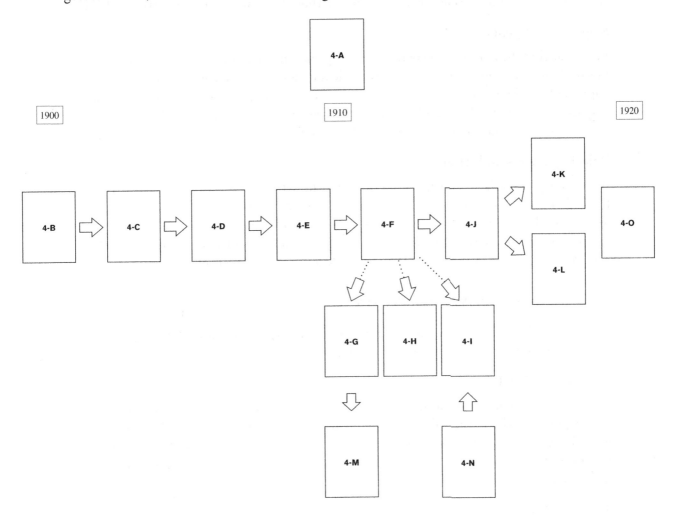

CRITICAL THINKING SKILLS

The activity sheets in this unit address various critical thinking skills. In addition, the constructed timeline emphasizes the essential critical thinking skills of identifying main ideas and details, sequencing events, and relating causes and effects.

Identifying Main Ideas and Details

Point out that Activity Sheet 4-A outlines the main ideas of the unit. Explain that the topics of the other activity sheets in the unit reflect the main ideas of the historical period the students are studying. Further explain that some activity sheets focus on the details related to specific topics.

As you and the students construct the timeline, show them that Activity Sheet 4-F focuses on a main idea while Activity Sheets 4-G, 4-H, 4-I, 4-M, and 4-N address the details. Have the students annotate the Timeline Arrows appropriately. Challenge the students to find similar relationships or create them by rearranging the activity sheets.

Sequencing Events

Point out that the activity sheets that make up the timeline are sequential. Show the students how the Timeline Dates provide a concrete reference for when events happened and how they relate to other events. (For example, the Treaty of Versailles was signed in 1919 before the League of Nations was created in 1920.) Make sure the students see that the Timeline Arrows indicate a chronological flow from left to right.

Relating Causes and Effects

As you and the students construct the timeline, show them that Activity Sheets 4-B through 4-F form a cause-and-effect chain. Also point out that Activity Sheet 4-F focuses on the cause of the effects addressed on Activity Sheets 4-J through 4-L. Have the students annotate the Timeline Arrows appropriately. Challenge the students to find similar relationships or create them by rearranging the activity sheets.

INDIVIDUAL ACTIVITY SHEET NOTES

The notes below provide a variety of tips on how to guide the students through the completion and extension of each activity sheet.

4-A. World War I

This activity is most appropriate for the students to complete with partners, in small groups, or as a whole class. For example, you might want to complete the questions with the whole class at the beginning of the unit and then have the students answer the questions at the end of the unit. Encourage the students to think of additional questions related to the topic.

4-B. War Clouds Over Europe

Emphasize that militarism, expansionism, nationalism, and alliances were long-term causes of the war that continued to increase tensions for many years.

4-C. The Assassination of Archduke Ferdinand

Present this event as a precipitative cause of the war, or as the spark that ignited the fire in Europe.

4-D. The Allies and the Central Powers

Ask the students to list only the major participants on each side. Encourage the students to memorize the countries that were involved.

4-E. A Voice From the Past: Woodrow Wilson

This excerpt gives a fair sense of Wilson's war message to Congress, but it does not include his mention of the Zimmermann telegram (he did not use the term). It also excludes his moving description of the great expenditures in men and material which Wilson expected that winning the war would take.

4-F. Major Events of World War I

Make sure the students include both military and political events.

4-G. Trench Warfare

Explain that trenches were dug as a means to escape enemy fire and that they spread as combatants continually tried to outflank each other. It was theoretically possible, one historian has pointed out, to walk the nearly 450 miles of the front staying in trenches the whole time. Try to help the students understand the horror of no-man's-land and the misery of living (and dying) in a trench.

4-H. New Weapons

Some of the weapons, notably the tank and poison gas, were employed to try to break the war of attrition that developed along the trench lines. The machine gun was one of the main reasons the trenches were dug to begin with.

4-I. The Home Front

Emphasize the importance of wartime production during this conflict. For example, in one two-week period the British launched about four million shells—and that was not completely atypical. Artillery had become more important as a means to break through enemy trench lines.

4-J. The Treaty of Versailles

Point out that there were actually several treaties that ended the war (with different countries), but that this one, forged at the Paris Peace Conference, was the most important. Emphasize how harsh the Treaty of Versailles was, forcing Germany to accept blame, pay reparations, and so on. It was this severity, as well as the consequences, that helped Adolf Hitler find an audience in postwar Germany.

4-K. Map Study: Europe Before and After World War I

Challenge the students to identify countries that disappeared and new countries that were created. Have the students compare and contrast the maps on the activity sheet with a current map of Europe.

4-L. The League of Nations

Point out that Woodrow Wilson proposed a "general association of nations" as one of his Fourteen Points. Ironically, the United States never joined this association, called the League of Nations. This was largely a result of the "America first" thinking in foreign policy that evolved quickly in the aftermath of World War I.

4-M. Biography: Alvin York

Alvin York's accomplishments during the war are amazing by any standard. He killed 20 German soldiers and captured more than 130 others—by himself. His accomplishments are even more noteworthy because his religion had led him to seek exemption from the draft.

4-N. Time Machine: Popular Songs

Help the students identify the main points of the essay, which should be written in the left-hand circle of the Venn diagram.

4-O. A Postcard From the Past: The Liberty Memorial

Suggest that the students visit www.libertymemorialmuseum.org (the web site of the Liberty Memorial Museum) to gather more information about the memorial.

World War I

In the box below, draw a picture or attach a picture from a magazine or the Internet that represents American involvement in World War I. The picture can be of anything you think is appropriate.

Ask questions about American involvement in World War I. Then, answer them.

Question: WHO_____?

Answer:_____

Question: WHAT_____?

Answer:_____

Question: WHERE _____?

Answer:_____

Question: WHEN _____?

Answer:_____

Question: WHY_____?

Answer:_____

Question: HOW_____?

Answer:_____

This important date in American history is brought to you by

_____

★ **Early 1900s** ★ War Clouds Over Europe

Define each term below. Then, explain how each one helped lead to the outbreak of war in Europe.

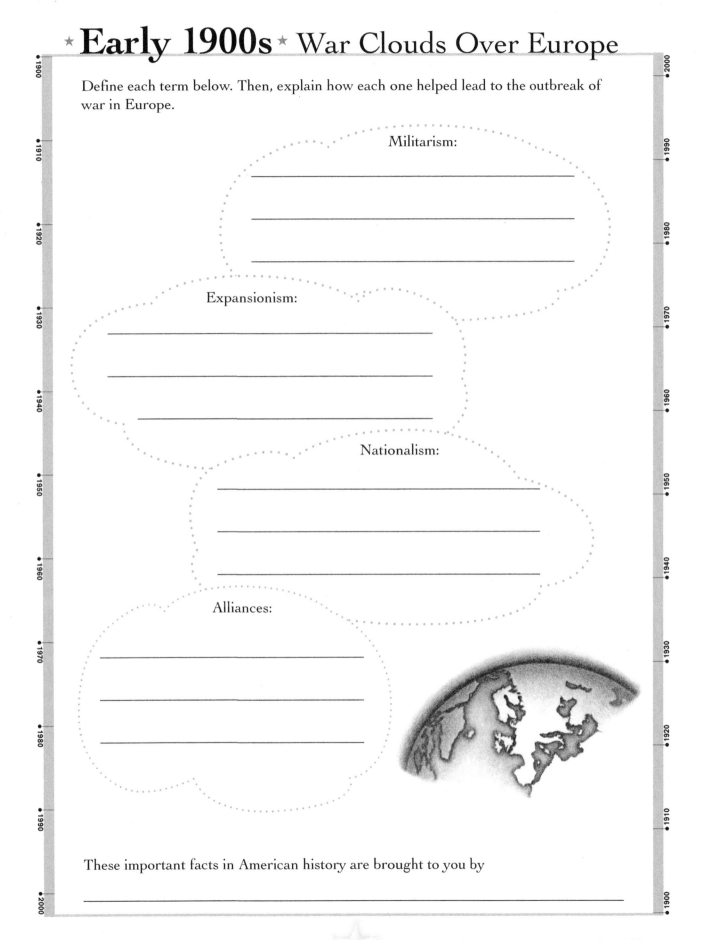

Militarism:

_____

_____

_____

Expansionism:

_____

_____

_____

Nationalism:

_____

_____

_____

Alliances:

_____

_____

_____

These important facts in American history are brought to you by

_____

Study the illustration. Then, write a caption for
it that tells about the assassination of Archduke
Franz Ferdinand. Your caption should tell who
he was and how his assassination helped begin
World War I.

_____

_____

_____

_____

_____

_____

_____

_____

_____

_____

_____

_____

This important date in American history is brought to you by

_____

List the major countries that made up the two sides that fought each other at the beginning of World War I.

World War I

ALLIES

CENTRAL POWERS

This important date in American history is brought to you by

_____

On April 2, 1917, President Woodrow Wilson called for Congress to declare war against Germany. Read the excerpts from his speech below. Then, answer the questions.

"[It has been Germany's] purpose to put aside all restraints of law or of humanity and use its submarines to sink every vessel that sought to approach either the ports of Great Britain and Ireland or the western coasts of Europe or any of the ports controlled by the enemies of Germany within the Mediterranean...Vessels of every kind, whatever their flag, their character, their cargo, their destination, their errand, have been ruthlessly sent to the bottom without warning and without thought of help or mercy for those on board...Even hospital ships...have been sunk with the same reckless lack of compassion or of principle...

Property can be paid for; the lives of peaceful and innocent people cannot be. The present German submarine warfare against commerce is a warfare against mankind. It is a war against all nations...The challenge is to all mankind. Each nation must decide for itself how it will meet it...[A]rmed neutrality [for the United States], it now appears, is impracticable...

With a profound sense of the solemn and even tragical character of the step I am taking...I advise that the Congress declare the recent course of the Imperial German Government to be in fact nothing less than war against the Government and people of the United States...and that it take immediate steps not only to put the country in a more thorough state of defense but also to exert all its power and employ all its resources to bring the Government of the German Empire to terms and end the war...

The world must be made safe for democracy."

What change in American policy was Wilson advocating?

_____

_____

What reason for this change did he give?

_____

_____

This important date in American history is brought to you by

_____

Major Events of World War I

Complete the timeline below.

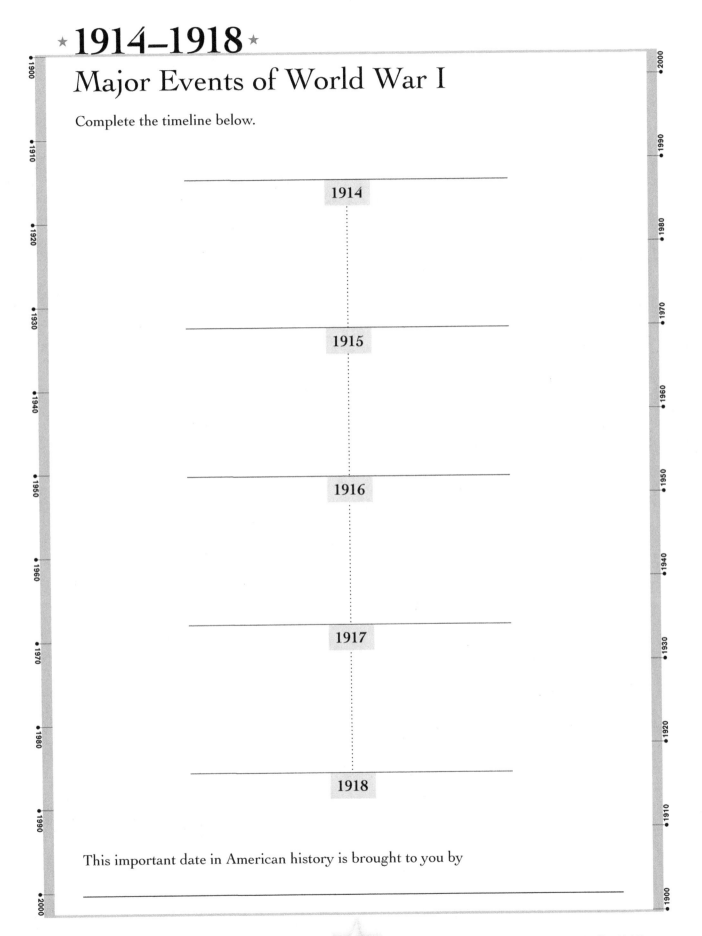

1914

1915

1916

1917

1918

This important date in American history is brought to you by

_____

★ 1914–1918 ★ Trench Warfare

Study the illustration below. Then, write a caption for it that tells about trench warfare during World War I. Your caption should tell what trench warfare was and describe what it was like for the soldiers.

_____

_____

_____

_____

_____

_____

This important date in American history is brought to you by

_____

New and dramatically improved weapons helped make World War I the deadliest war the world had ever seen. Identify each weapon below. Then, tell something about it.

_____

_____

_____

_____

_____

_____

_____

_____

_____

_____

_____

_____

This important date in American history is brought to you by

_____

Complete the diagram.

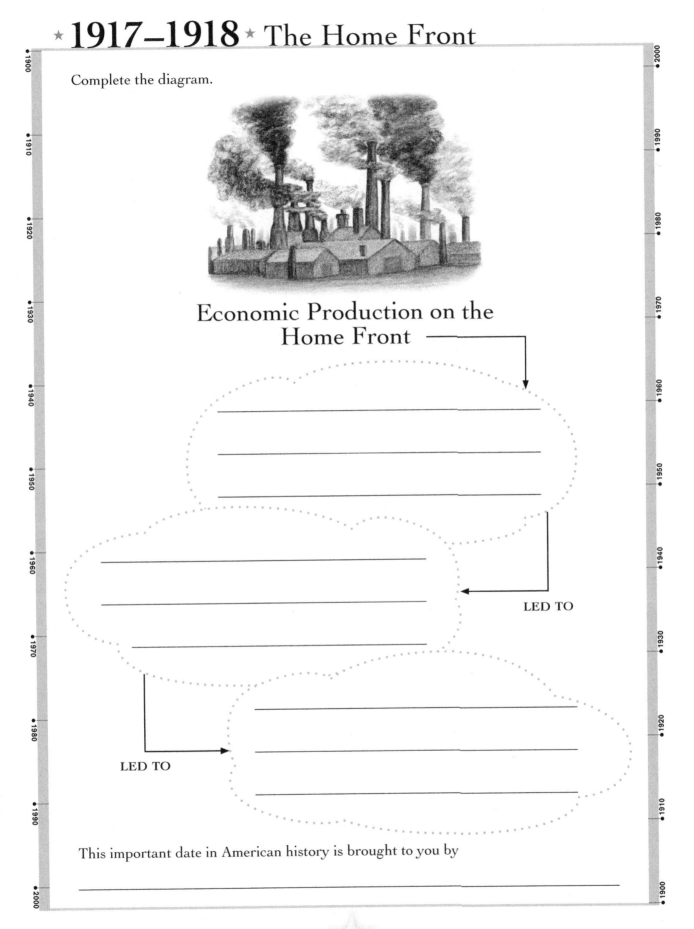

Economic Production on the Home Front

LED TO

LED TO

This important date in American history is brought to you by

_____

The Treaty of Versailles marked the effort to resolve the conflicts of World War I. List its major provisions or requirements.

The Treaty of Versailles

This important date in American history is brought to you by

_____

EUROPE IN 1914, JUST BEFORE WORLD WAR I

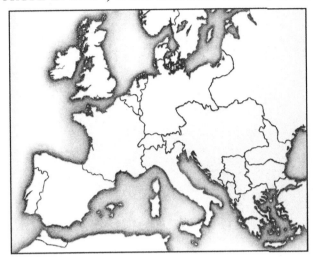

EUROPE IN 1919, JUST AFTER WORLD WAR I

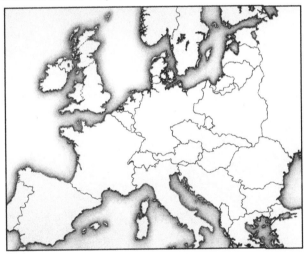

Write a short paragraph that summarizes how World War I changed the map of Europe.

_____

_____

_____

_____

This important idea in American history is brought to you by

_____

★ 1920 ★ The League of Nations

Complete the chart below.

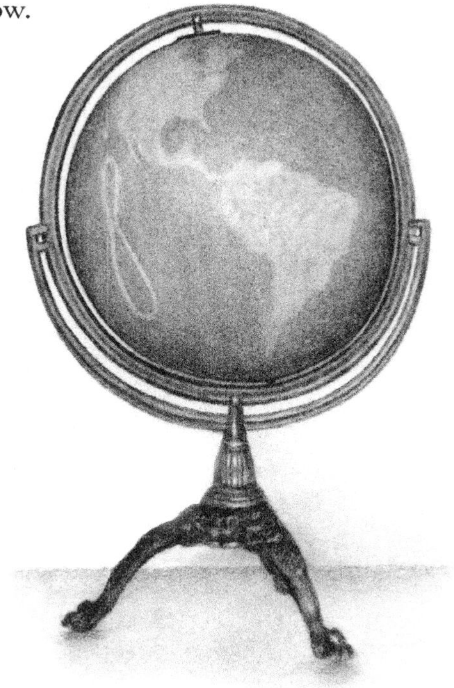

The League of Nations

What It Was	
What Its Purpose Was	
Who Proposed It	
Why the United States Didn't Join	
What Organization Replaced It	

This important date in American history is brought to you by

____

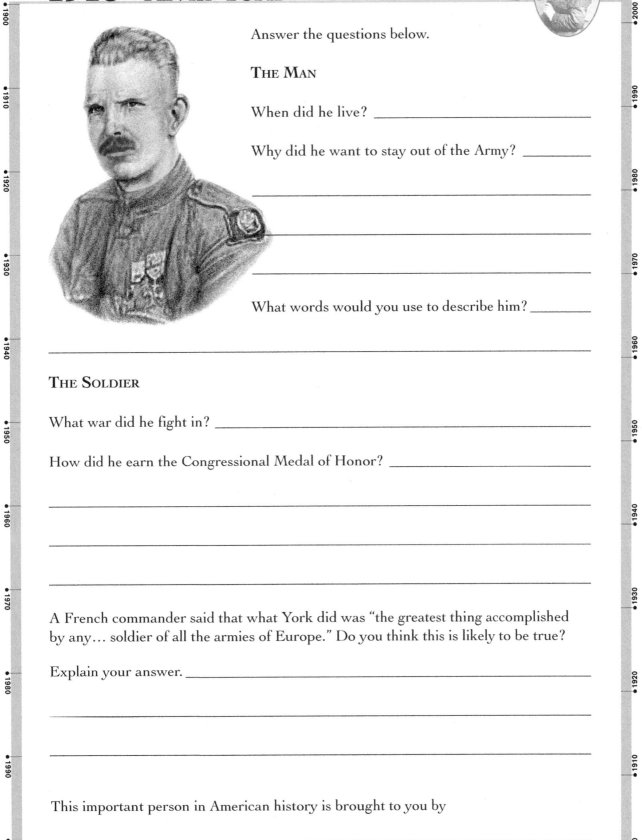

Answer the questions below.

THE MAN

When did he live? _____

Why did he want to stay out of the Army? _____

_____

_____

_____

What words would you use to describe him? _____

_____

THE SOLDIER

What war did he fight in? _____

How did he earn the Congressional Medal of Honor? _____

_____

_____

_____

A French commander said that what York did was "the greatest thing accomplished by any... soldier of all the armies of Europe." Do you think this is likely to be true?

Explain your answer. _____

_____

_____

This important person in American history is brought to you by

_____

Activate the Time Machine to learn about popular songs during the World
War I era. In the left-hand circle, write facts about popular songs during that time.
In the right-hand circle, write facts about popular songs today. In the space where the
circles overlap, write facts about popular songs that both time periods have in common.

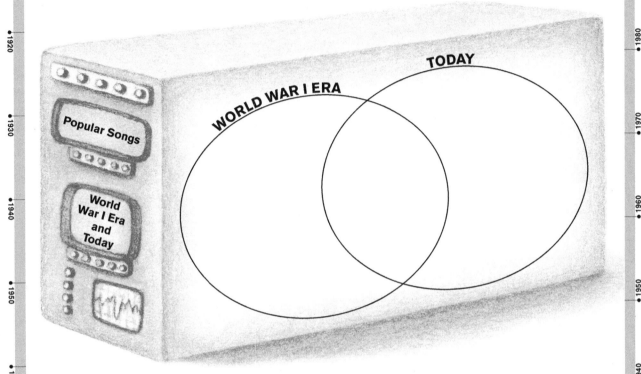

Popular songs during the World War I era were sung more than they were listened
to. There were no radios to speak of, and not everyone had a phonograph. Typically,
people enjoyed the latest tunes during family sing-alongs, often accompanied by a piano.

People rushed to the store to get the latest songs—not on CD, but on sheet music.
Most of the songs had a patriotic message. The most popular songwriter, George
M. Cohan, wrote favorites like, "You're a Grand Old Flag," "I'm a Yankee Doodle
Dandy," and "Over There," which became an unofficial theme song for the war.

A few songs protested the war, but more songs were about the sadness of separation
from loved ones during wartime. Still, there is no denying that the most popular
songs were those that celebrated the United States and the war.

This important trip into American history is brought to you by

_____

★ The Liberty Memorial ★

The Liberty Memorial in Kansas City, Missouri, was erected soon after World War I "in honor of those who served in the world war in defense of liberty and our country." Its over 200-foot tall Memorial Tower is topped by four statues representing courage, honor, patriotism, and sacrifice. What is it like to visit there? Conduct research to find out.

Use the Internet or any other resources your teacher suggests. Read the articles and study the illustrations. When you have gathered enough information, make a postcard.

On the front of the postcard, draw a picture or attach a picture from a magazine or the Internet that gives some information about the Liberty Memorial. On the back of the postcard, write a caption that explains the picture. Then, write a note to a friend that tells about things to do and see at the site.

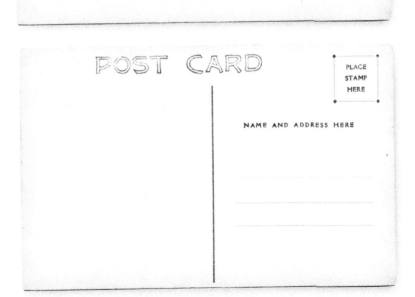

This important place in American history is brought to you by

Unit 5 The Roaring Twenties and the Great Depression

1920–1940

Unit Overview

The 1920s and 1930s reflect the highs and lows of a capitalistic economy. The prosperity of the 1920s turned—suddenly, it seemed—into the abject misery of the 1930s. The net result of these highs and lows was a reshaping of America into something very much like what we know today.

Activity Sheet 5-A provides a unit overview. Activity Sheet 5-B takes a look at the United States in geographic and demographic terms—the latter remarkable for the shift of the United States from a rural to an urban society. Activity Sheets 5-C through 5-G highlight the major economic and social developments of the Roaring Twenties— the economic boom, the embracing of new consumer goods, and the new roles of American women during this decade.

The boom soon went bust, of course, and the students consider why on Activity Sheet 5-H. Activity Sheet 5-I provides an overview of the Great Depression. The harsh realities of Depression-era life are the subjects of Activity Sheets 5-J through 5-L. Activity Sheets 5-M and 5-N address the Roosevelt administration's response to the Great Depression, as well as Roosevelt himself.

The Time Machine, Activity Sheet 5-O, compares women's fashions today to women's fashions during the 1920s and 1930s. A Postcard From the Past, Activity Sheet 5-P, is about the Franklin Delano Roosevelt Memorial.

Focus Activities

To focus the students' attention on this period of American history, consider the following activities:

Because They Roared

Ask the students why the 1920s are often called the Roaring Twenties. Make sure the students understand that the term does not only refer to the economic boom of the decade but also to the lifestyle of many Americans during that time. Discuss the popularity of flappers, automobile racing, and stunts.

The Almighty Auto

Have the students list at least five ways the United States would be radically different without automobiles. Record the responses on the board. Explain that "automania" first took hold in the 1920s.

A Classroom Visitor

Invite someone who lived through the Great Depression to share his or her memories with the class. Emphasize that the Great Depression was not an abstract historical event but rather a devastating reality for most Americans.

CONSTRUCTING THE TIMELINE

This unit consists of 16 activity sheets that focus on significant events, people, and places related to the Roaring Twenties and the Great Depression. Each activity sheet is designed to, once completed, become part of a posted classroom timeline of the period covered in the unit.

The Introduction (pages VII–XIII) provides a detailed explanation of how to use the activity sheets in the classroom and suggests various ways to construct the timeline using the completed activity sheets.

You can construct the timeline any way you see fit. Use the Timeline Components (pages XVIII–XXV) to connect the activity sheets. Below are two possible timelines, constructed from the activity sheets in this unit and the Timeline Components.

Option 1: Basic Timeline

Construct this timeline to identify only the essential elements of the period.

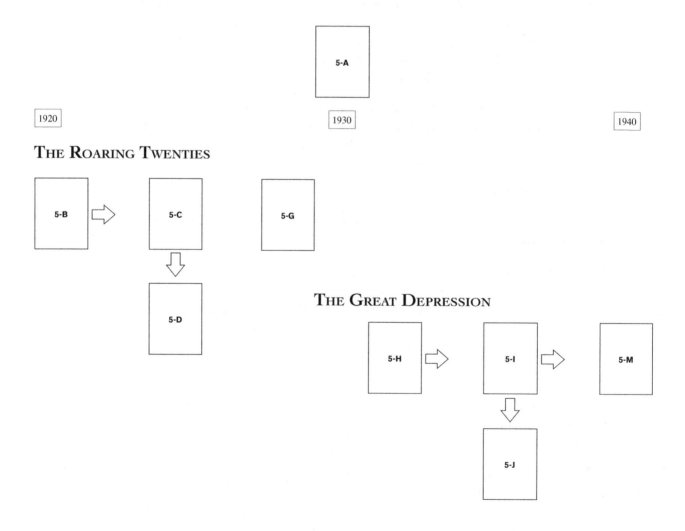

Option 2: Complete Timeline

Construct this timeline to identify the essential elements of the period, examine them in greater detail, and extend student learning.

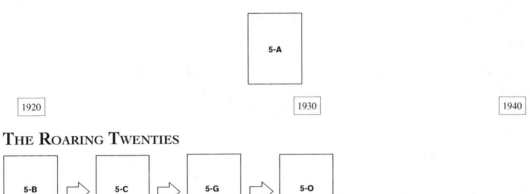

5-A

1920   1930   1940

THE ROARING TWENTIES

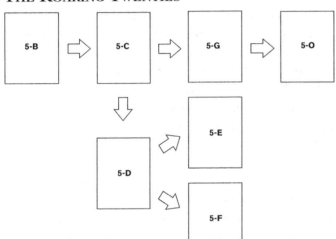

5-B → 5-C → 5-G → 5-O

5-D → 5-E

5-D → 5-F

THE GREAT DEPRESSION

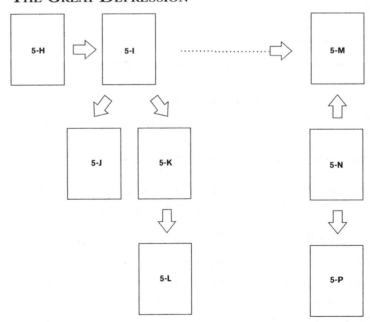

5-H → 5-I ·········· → 5-M

5-J   5-K   5-N

5-K → 5-L

5-N → 5-P

CRITICAL THINKING SKILLS

The activity sheets in this unit address various critical thinking skills. In addition, the constructed timeline emphasizes the essential critical thinking skills of identifying main ideas and details, sequencing events, and relating causes and effects.

Identifying Main Ideas and Details

Point out that Activity Sheet 5-A outlines the main ideas of the unit. Explain that the topics of the other activity sheets in the unit reflect the main ideas of the historical period the students are studying. Further explain that some activity sheets focus on the details related to specific topics.

As you and the students construct the timeline, show them that the first subheading is a main idea while Activity Sheets 5-B through 5-G and Activity Sheet 5-O focus on details. Point out the similar relationship between the second subheading and Activity Sheets 5-H through 5-N and Activity Sheet 5-P. Also explain that Activity Sheet 5-I forms a main idea while Activity Sheets 5-J through 5-L focus on details. Have the students annotate the Timeline Arrows appropriately. Challenge the students to find similar relationships or create them by rearranging the activity sheets.

Sequencing Events

Point out that the activity sheets that make up the timeline are sequential. Show the students how the Timeline Dates provide a concrete reference for when events happened and how they relate to other events. (For example, the economic boom of the 1920s happened before the Great Depression of the 1930s.) Make sure the students see that the Timeline Arrows indicate a chronological flow from left to right. Also, point out that this unit's timeline has two basic layers that are separated by subheadings.

Relating Causes and Effects

As you and the students construct the timeline, show them that the following activity sheets form cause/effect relationships: 5-C/5-D, 5-E, 5-F; 5-G/5-O; 5-H/5-I; and 5-I/5-M. Have the students annotate the Timeline Arrows appropriately. Challenge the students to find similar relationships or create them by rearranging the activity sheets.

INDIVIDUAL ACTIVITY SHEET NOTES

The notes below provide a variety of tips on how to guide the students through the completion and extension of each activity sheet.

5-A. The Roaring Twenties and the Great Depression

This activity is most appropriate for the students to complete with partners, in small groups, or as a whole class. For example, you might want to complete the questions with the whole class at the beginning of the unit and then have the students answer the questions at the end of the unit. Encourage the students to think of additional questions related to the topic.

5-B. Map Study: The United States in 1920

Point out that the demographic data on this activity sheet marked a turning point in American history. For the first time, more Americans lived in urban areas than in rural ones.

5-C. The Economic Boom

Emphasize the role that the mass-producing automobile industry and related industries and businesses (for example, gasoline, steel, and tourism) played in the economic boom. Tell the students that farmers and laborers did not share the good fortune.

5-D. New Consumer Goods

Point out that many of these devices are commonplace today and that the American home of the 1920s was beginning to resemble the American home of today.

5-E. The Impact of the Automobile

It is almost impossible to overstate the effects automobiles have had on American life—both good and bad. Extend this activity sheet by having the students categorize the effects they listed as good or bad.

5-F. The Radio and Movies

Ask the students to explain how the radio and movies helped "shrink" the country, and the world, for Americans. Explain that this is another example of how the United States in the 1920s was becoming more like the country the students live in today.

5-G. New Roles for Women

Make sure the students include the ratification of the nineteenth amendment, guaranteeing women's suffrage.

5-H. Causes of the Great Depression

Like most historical events, the Great Depression did not have a single cause. The primary factors in making this depression so devastating were protectionism, speculation, urbanization, and economic inequality.

5-I. The Great Depression

Encourage the students to memorize these facts. Have the students compare and contrast Hoover's and Roosevelt's responses to the economic calamity.

5-J. Life During the Great Depression

Emphasize how truly distressing life was for many Americans. Unemployment, malnutrition, and homelessness were common; starvation was a real fear. The famous photographer Dorothea Lange took a picture of an exhausted woman holding a baby with two young children resting on her sides. Lange's notes regarding the photograph read, "They had been living on [unmarketable] vegetables from the...fields and birds that the children killed. She had just sold the tires from her car to buy food." This was the reality for millions of people during the Great Depression.

5-K. Map Study: The Dust Bowl

Tell the students that for a long time the Dust Bowl was thought to have been caused simply by drought. Explain that scientists have determined that the Dust Bowl was actually caused to a large degree by the replacement of millions of acres of natural vegetation by plowed earth.

5-L. A Voice From the Past: John Steinbeck

Encourage the students to read all of *The Grapes of Wrath*. Explain that, although a fictional novel, the book is quite accurate in describing what life was really like for the Okies in the Dust Bowl.

5-M. The New Deal

Emphasize the fundamental change in the role of government that the New Deal was. It marked a shift from a more hands-off approach to the economy and social problems to an approach of increasing government participation in many aspects of life. Point out how many New Deal programs, like Social Security and the Tennessee Valley Authority (TVA), are still in effect today. Point out too that the debate in this country about how large a role the government should play still continues.

5-N. Biography: Franklin Delano Roosevelt

Have the students answer similar questions about Franklin Delano Roosevelt's remarkable wife, Eleanor Roosevelt.

5-O. Time Machine: Women's Fashions

Help the students identify the main points of the essay, which should be written in the left-hand circle of the Venn diagram.

5-P. A Postcard From the Past: Franklin Delano Roosevelt Memorial

Suggest that the students visit www.nps.gov (the web site of the National Park Service) to gather information about the Franklin Delano Roosevelt Memorial.

Twenties and the Great Depression

In the box below, draw a picture or attach a picture from a magazine or the Internet that represents one of these periods of American history. The picture can be of anything you think is appropriate.

Ask questions about one of these periods of American history. Then, answer them.

Question: WHO_____?

Answer:_____

Question: WHAT_____?

Answer:_____

Question: WHERE _____?

Answer:_____

Question: WHEN _____?

Answer:_____

Question: WHY _____?

Answer:_____

Question: HOW_____?

Answer:_____

This important date in American history is brought to you by

_____

Label the following items on the map below: states in 1920, several major cities, and major bodies of water.

Fill in the missing information below. Record the total population, and shade the circle graph to illustrate the rural/urban distribution.

THE UNITED STATES IN **1920**

Total Population: _____

Rural/Urban Distribution: _____

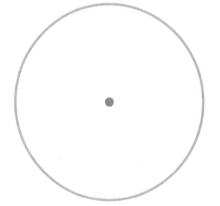

This important date in American history is brought to you by

_____

★ 1920s ★ The Economic Boom

Complete the diagram below to show the main causes of the economic boom of the 1920s.

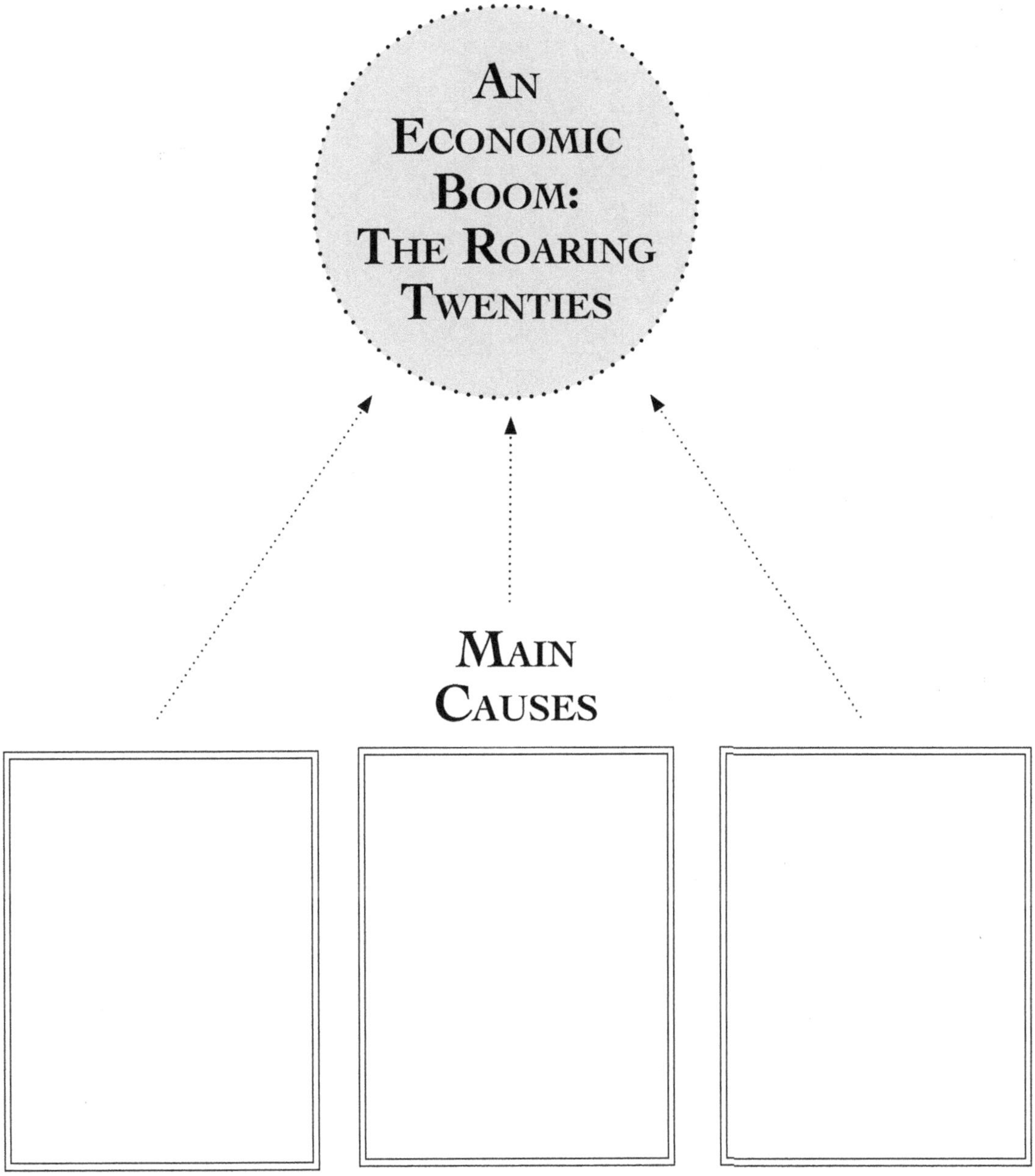

An Economic Boom: The Roaring Twenties
Main Causes

These important facts in American history are brought to you by

____

★ 1920s ★ New Consumer Goods

Many new consumer products became popular in the 1920s. Draw and label several of them to "furnish" the house below.

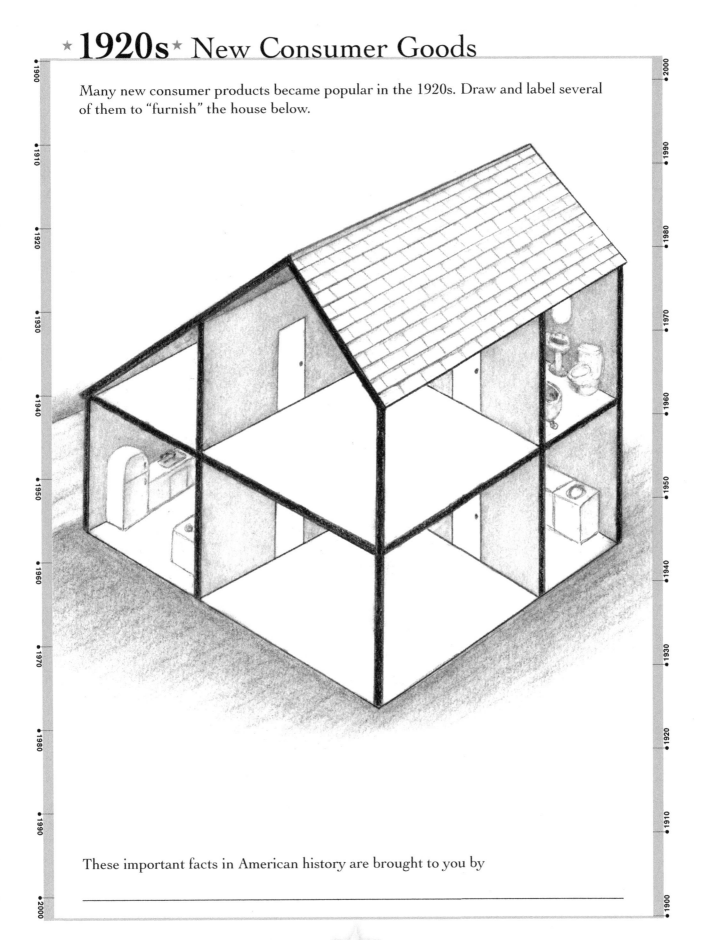

These important facts in American history are brought to you by

_____

★ **1920s** ★ The Impact of the Automobile

In 1920, there were about nine million cars and trucks on American roads, one vehicle for every 13 Americans. By the end of the 1920s, there were about 27 million cars, or about one car for every five Americans. Most of the cars were the Model T. More than 15 million of this model were sold by Henry Ford and his company.

Fill in the "billboards" below with ways the automobile affected America in the 1920s.

These important facts in American history are brought to you by

_____

Write three important facts about the radio and three about movies during the 1920s.

THE RADIO

_____

_____

_____

MOVIES

_____

_____

_____

These important facts in American history are brought to you by

_____

★ **1920s** ★ New Roles for Women

List at least three ways life changed for American women during the 1920s.

1920s FLAPPER

These important facts in American history are brought to you by

_____

Complete the diagram below to show the main causes of the Great Depression of the 1930s.

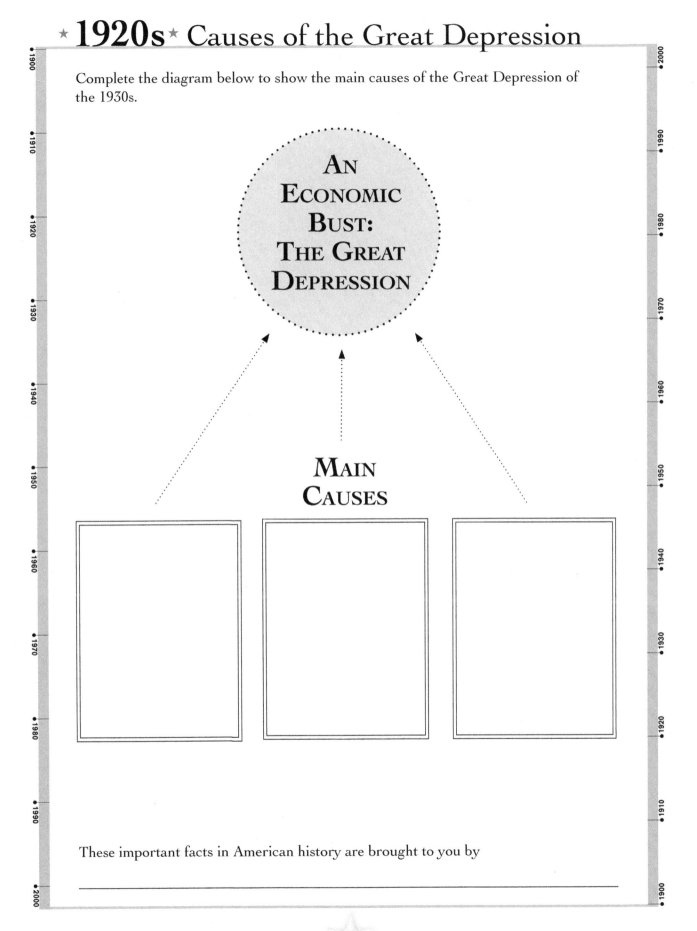

AN ECONOMIC BUST: THE GREAT DEPRESSION

MAIN CAUSES

These important facts in American history are brought to you by

_____

Complete the fact sheet below.

FACT SHEET: THE GREAT DEPRESSION

What It Was: _____

_____

_____

When It Happened: _____

Who the American Presidents Were: _____

What Areas It Affected the Most: _____

_____

_____

These important facts in American history are brought to you by

_____

Study the illustration below. Then, write a caption for it that tells about life during the Great Depression. Your caption should tell how the Great Depression affected Americans and how they coped with these hardships.

_____

_____

_____

_____

_____

_____

This important fact in American history is brought to you by

_____

Shade and label the Dust Bowl on the map. Then, answer the questions below.

What caused the Dust Bowl? _____

_____

How did it affect farmers? _____

_____

Who were the Okies? _____

_____

What ended the Dust Bowl? _____

_____

These important facts in American history are brought to you by

_____

John Steinbeck's novel *The Grapes of Wrath* tells of the hardships faced by the Okies during the Great Depression. Read the excerpt from the novel below. Then, answer the questions.

"...And a homeless hungry man, driving the roads with his wife beside him and his thin children in the back seat, could look at the fallow fields which might produce food but not profit and that man could know how a fallow field is a sin and the unused land a crime against the thin children. And such a man drove along the roads and knew temptation at every field, and knew the lust to take these fields and make them grow strength for his children and a little comfort for his wife. The temptation was before him always. The fields goaded him, and the company ditches with good water flowing were a goad to him.

And in the south he saw the golden oranges hanging on the trees, the little golden oranges on the dark green trees; and guards with shotguns patrolling the lines so a man might not pick an orange for a thin child, oranges to be dumped if the price was low.

He drove his old car into a town. He scoured the farms for work. Where can we sleep the night?

Well, there's a Hooverville on the edge of the river. There's a whole raft of Okies there.

He drove his old car to Hooverville. He never asked again, for there was a Hooverville on the edge of every town.

The rag town lay close to water; and the houses were tents, and weed-thatched enclosures, paper houses, a great junk pile. The man drove his family in and became a citizen of Hooverville—always they were called Hooverville. The man put up his own tent as near to water as he could get; or if he had no tent, he went to the city dump and brought back cartons and built a house of corrugated paper. And when the rains came the house melted and washed away. He settled in Hooverville and he scoured the countryside for work, and the little money he had went for gasoline to look for work. In the evening the men gathered and talked together...they talked of the land they had seen...."

What was a Hooverville? _____

_____

What adjectives would you use to describe life for Okies during the Great Depression?

_____

_____

This important date in American history is brought to you by

_____

★ 1933 ★ The New Deal

Follow the directions and answer the questions below.

Name the President who enacted the New Deal. _____

Explain what the New Deal was. _____

_____

Why was the New Deal enacted? _____

Describe the Civilian Conservation Corps. _____

_____

Explain what Social Security is. _____

_____

Answer this question: What is the Tennessee Valley Authority? _____

_____

List some other New Deal programs. _____

_____

This important date in American history is brought to you by

_____

Franklin Delano Roosevelt

Answer the questions below.

THE MAN

When did he live? _____

What do we know about his early life? _____

_____

What disease did he cope with?_____

_____

What words would you use to describe him? _____

_____

HIS PRESIDENCY

When did he serve as President? _____

What major historical events took place during his presidency? _____

_____

What were his major accomplishments?_____

_____

Explain the following statement made by President Roosevelt: "The only thing we have to fear is fear itself." _____

_____

_____

This important person in American history is brought to you by

_____

★ Women's Fashions ★

Activate the Time Machine to learn about women's fashions during the 1920s. In the left-hand circle, write facts about women's fashions during that time. In the right-hand circle, write facts about women's fashions today. In the space where the circles overlap, write facts about clothing that both time periods have in common.

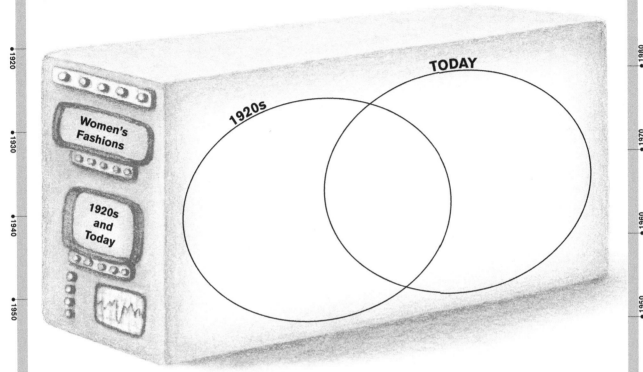

By about 1920, most women began to wear ready-to-wear clothing. That is, instead of being custom-made, clothing consisted of mass-produced items that women purchased in stores or from catalogs. This made fashionable clothes less expensive, and more people could afford them. Still, many women continued to make their own clothes, following store-bought patterns of the latest designs.

Dresses, which had traditionally been worn at ankle length or longer, were worn shorter, at the knee or calf. Fashionable dresses hung straight and were not fitted close to the body. Small, close-fitted hats called "cloches" were popular. They went well with the short hairstyles that were in fashion during the decade.

Women also began wearing more makeup during the 1920s. In part, this was a result of a demand created by advertising.

This important trip into American history is brought to you by

_____

★ Franklin Delano Roosevelt Memorial ★

The Franklin Delano Roosevelt Memorial stands in the nation's capital, Washington, D.C. What is it like to visit there? Conduct research to find out.

Use the Internet or any other resources your teacher suggests. Read the articles and study the illustrations. When you have gathered enough information, make a postcard.

On the front of the postcard, draw a picture or attach a picture from a magazine or the Internet that gives some information about the Franklin Delano Roosevelt Memorial. On the back of the postcard, write a caption that explains the picture. Then, write a note to a friend that tells about things to do and see at the site.

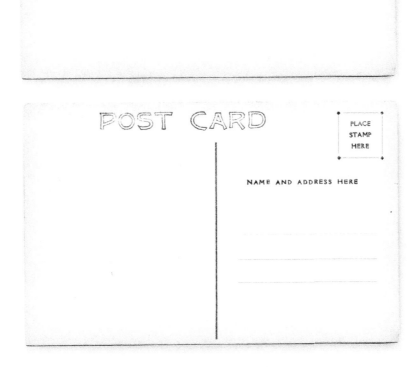

POST CARD

PLACE
STAMP
HERE

NAME AND ADDRESS HERE

This important place in American history is brought to you by

_____

UNIT 6 World War II

1930–1950

UNIT OVERVIEW

It is difficult to overstate the importance of World War II in shaping the world we live in today. Tens of millions died, the Holocaust brought a nightmare to life, maps were redrawn around the globe, anticolonial movements gained way, the nuclear age began, and two superpowers emerged that would soon bring the world to the brink of destruction.

Activity Sheet 6-A provides a unit overview. Activity Sheets 6-B through 6-D summarize the primary reasons for World War II. Activity Sheets 6-E through 6-H are designed to give the students an overview of the greatest war in history, including main ideas about the war, major events of the war, the impact of the war on life in the United States, and the weapons that helped win the war.

Activity Sheets 6-I and 6-J introduce the students to two of the most remarkable American figures to come out of the war: the courageous Audie Murphy and the humane Ernie Pyle. Activity Sheets 6-K through 6-M discuss the conclusion of the war and its aftermath.

Activity Sheet 6-N takes a geopolitical and demographic look at the United States in 1950.

The Time Machine, Activity Sheet 6-O, compares shopping today to shopping in the 1940s. A Postcard From the Past, Activity Sheet 6-P, is about the National World War II Memorial.

FOCUS ACTIVITIES

To focus the students' attention on this period of American history, consider the following activities:

A Veteran

Invite a veteran of World War II, or another American with vivid recollections of the home front, to share some of his or her experiences with the students.

Working Women

Ask the students if they know who "Rosie the Riveter" was. Explain this popular World War II image, and tell the students that working women during this time were pioneers. Point out that World War II, in many ways, led to the acceptance of women in the workforce today.

See Any Good Movies Lately?

Invite the students to tell about movies they have seen that were set during World War II. Help the students identify the realistic, historically accurate aspects of each movie.

CONSTRUCTING THE TIMELINE

This unit consists of 16 activity sheets that focus on significant events, people, and places related to the World War II era. Each activity sheet is designed to, once completed, become part of a posted classroom timeline of the period covered in the unit.

The introduction (pages VII–XIII) provides a detailed discussion of how to use the activity sheets in the classroom and suggests various ways to construct the timeline using completed activity sheets.

You can construct the timeline any way you see fit. Use the Timeline Components (pages XVIII–XXV) to connect the activity sheets. Below are two possible timelines, constructed from the activity sheets in this unit and the Timeline Components.

Option 1: Basic Timeline

Construct this timeline to identify only the essential elements of the period.

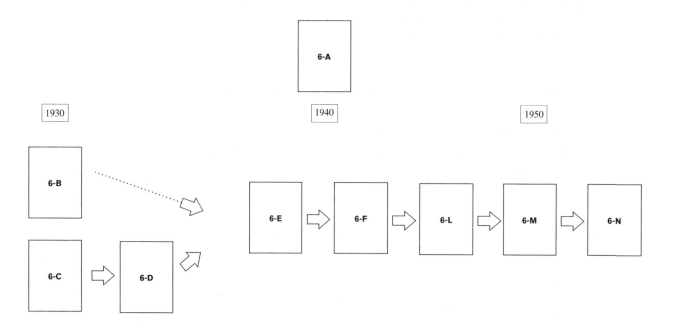

Option 2: Complete Timeline

Construct this timeline to identify the essential elements of the period, examine them in greater detail, and extend student learning.

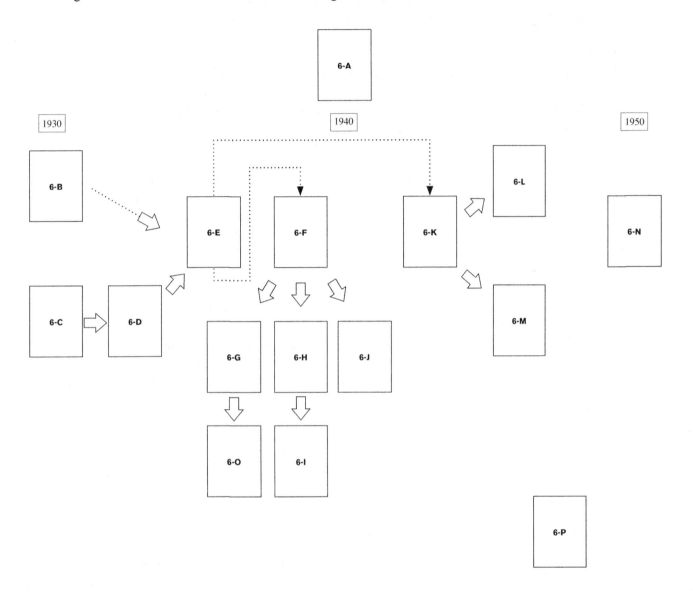

CRITICAL THINKING SKILLS

The activity sheets in this unit address various critical thinking skills. In addition, the constructed timeline emphasizes the essential critical thinking skills of identifying main ideas and details, sequencing events, and relating causes and effects.

Identifying Main Ideas and Details

Point out that Activity Sheet 6-A outlines the main ideas of the unit. Explain that the topics of the other activity sheets in the unit reflect the main ideas of the historical period the students are studying. Further explain that some activity sheets focus on the details related to specific topics.

As you and the students construct the timeline, show them that Activity Sheet 6-E forms a main idea and Activity Sheets 6-F through 6-J, and Activity Sheet 6-O, focus on details. Also point out that the following activity sheets form main idea/detail relationships: 6-D/6-E, 6-G/6-O, and 6-H/6-I. Have the students annotate the Timeline Arrows appropriately. Challenge the students to find similar relationships or create them by rearranging the activity sheets.

Sequencing Events

Point out that the activity sheets that make up the timeline are sequential. Show the students how the Timeline Dates provide a concrete reference for when events happened and how they relate to other events. (For example, World War II began in 1939 before the United Nations was formed in 1945.) Make sure the students see that the Timeline Arrows indicate a chronological flow from left to right.

Relating Causes and Effects

As you and the students construct the timeline, show them that the following activity sheets form cause/effect relationships: 6-B, 6-C, 6-D/6-E; 6-H/6-K; and 6-L/6-M. Have the students annotate the Timeline Arrows appropriately. Challenge the students to find similar relationships or create them by rearranging the activity sheets.

INDIVIDUAL ACTIVITY SHEET NOTES

The notes below provide a variety of tips on how to guide the students through the completion and extension of each activity sheet.

6-A. World War II

This activity is most appropriate for the students to complete with partners, in small groups, or as a whole class. For example, you might want to complete the questions with the whole class at the beginning of the unit and then have the students answer the questions at the end of the unit. Encourage the students to think of additional questions related to the topic.

6-B. Changes in Italy and Germany

This activity sheet provides a good opportunity to discuss the Holocaust with the students. Make sure they understand that Hitler was embraced by a Germany humiliated and economically devastated by its loss in World War I.

6-C. Japanese Expansionism

Some students might find this activity sheet easier to complete if they expand each question word into a complete sentence before answering it. For example, "Why did the Japanese government follow a policy of expansionism?"

6-D. Pearl Harbor

Have the students memorize the date. Make sure they understand the Japanese motivation for the attack.

6-E. World War II: Main Ideas

Invite an American who lived during the World War II years to speak to the class. As an alternative, you might share appropriate excerpts from *The Good War*, by Studs Terkel. Make sure the students focus on major historical concepts. Explain that learning main ideas will give the students a context into which they can place the details they learn.

6-F. Major Events of World War II

You might want to have the students devote one side of the timeline to events in the war against Japan and the other side of the timeline to events in the war against Germany.

6-G. The Home Front

Point out that the massive war production effort helped lift the United States out of the Great Depression. Emphasize the vital role that women played.

6-H. Important American Weapons of World War II

In studying World War II, the fighting technology is often overlooked, yet it was critical to the American victory. You might want to share with the students the fact that American General George Patton called the M1 rifle "the greatest battle implement ever devised." You might also want to point out that the Higgins boat was nicknamed after the company that manufactured it. The boat's official designation was "Landing Craft, Vehicle, Personnel" (LCVP).

6-I. Biography: Audie Murphy

Encourage the students to read Murphy's *To Hell and Back* or view the movie of the same title.

6-J. A Voice From the Past: Ernie Pyle

Tell the students that Pyle was famous for his sympathy for the ordinary soldier. However, in this report, he underscores a less touching but essential fact about World War II: the ability to "afford" a vast industrial production of war material was essential to winning the war.

6-K. The End of the War and the Beginning of the Nuclear Age

Assign teams to conduct a debate about the decision to drop the atomic bomb. Have the students discuss whether they think it was immoral or whether they think it was justified.

6-L. Major Effects of World War II

Consider having the students classify their responses appropriately (for example, human effects, political effects, short-term effects, and long-term effects).

6-M. The United Nations

Consider introducing this activity sheet by showing the students a newspaper article about some current United Nations activities.

6-N. Map Study: The United States in 1950

Emphasize the growing population of the United States and its increasing urbanization.

6-O. Time Machine: Shopping

Help the students identify the main points of the essay, which should be written in the left-hand circle of the Venn diagram.

6-P. A Postcard From the Past: The National World War II Memorial

Suggest that the students visit www.nps.gov (the web site of the National Park Service) to gather information about the National World War II Memorial.

In the box below, draw a picture or attach a picture from a magazine or the Internet that represents this period of American history. The picture can be of anything you think is appropriate.

Ask questions about this period of American involvement in World War II. Then, answer them.

Question: WHO_____?

Answer:_____

Question: WHAT_____?

Answer:_____

Question: WHERE _____?

Answer:_____

Question: WHEN _____?

Answer:_____

Question: WHY_____?

Answer:_____

Question: HOW_____?

Answer:_____

This important date in American history is brought to you by

_____

Write short paragraphs that summarize developments in each of the two countries under these leaders.

ITALY UNDER BENITO MUSSOLINI

GERMANY UNDER ADOLF HITLER

These important people in American history are brought to you by

_____

★1930s★ Japanese Expansionism

Complete the diagram below by answering the questions about Japanese expansionism.

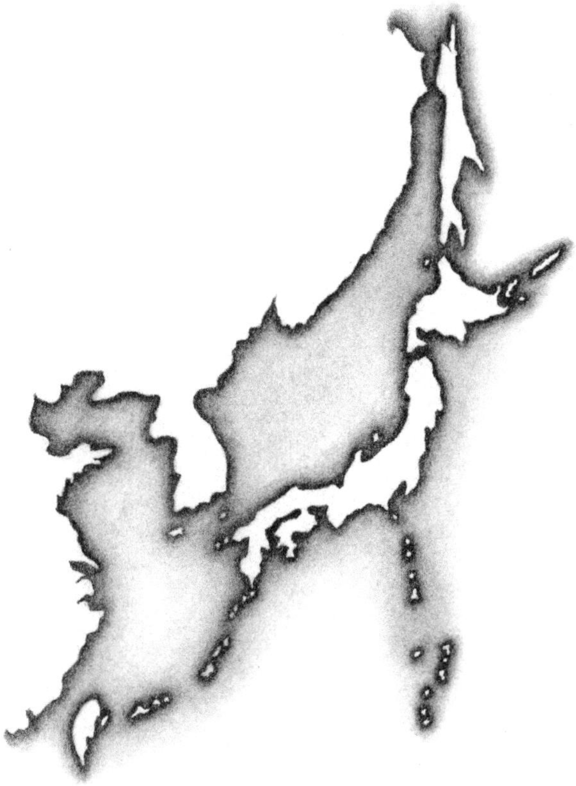

Where?

____

____

____

Why?

____

____

____

How?

____

____

____

Who?

____

____

____

When?

____

____

____

These important facts in American history are brought to you by

____

December 7, 1941 ★ Pearl Harbor

Study the illustration below. Then, write a caption for it that tells about the Japanese attack on Pearl Harbor. Your caption should tell why the attack was made, what its results were, and how the United States responded.

_____

_____

_____

_____

_____

_____

_____

This important date in American history is brought to you by

_____

★ 1939–1945 ★ World War II: Main Ideas

Complete the diagram below.

Main Reasons for the War

____
____
____
____
____
____

Main Countries That Fought in the War

Allies: ______________________
____
____

Axis: ______________________
____
____

World War II

Main Leaders

Allies: ______________________
____
____

Axis: ______________________
____
____

Main Results of the War

____
____
____
____
____
____

This important date in American history is brought to you by

____

Major Events of World War II

Complete the timeline below.

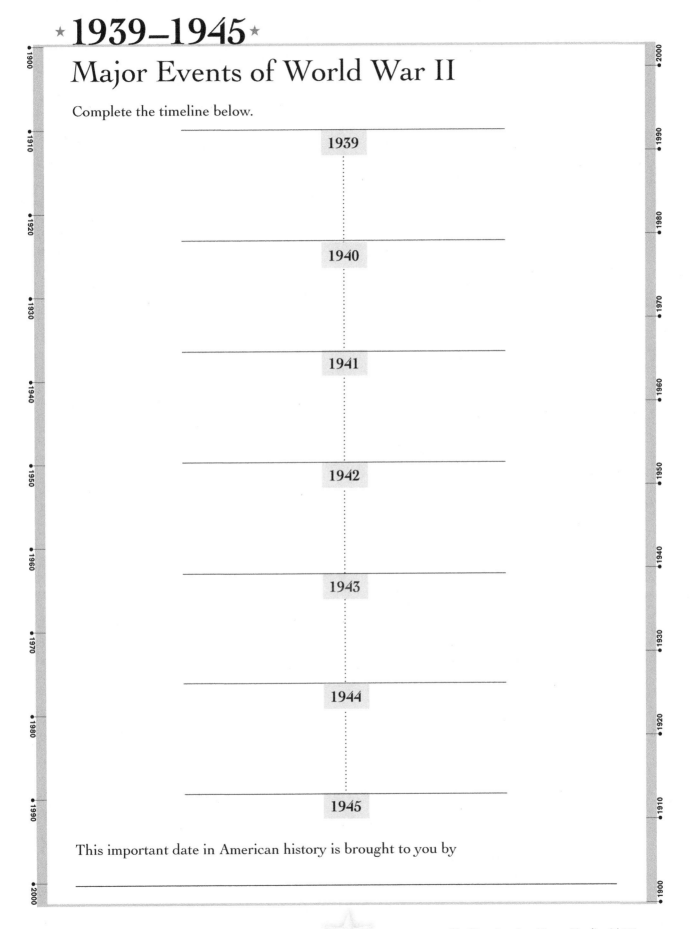

1939

1940

1941

1942

1943

1944

1945

This important date in American history is brought to you by

_____

Efforts on the home front played a vital role in the American victory in World War II.
Complete the diagram below by listing some of the effects of home front efforts.

HOME FRONT EFFORTS

Effects on the Economy	
Effects on the Workforce	
Effects on Consumers	

These important facts in American history are brought to you by

_____

★ 1941–1945 ★ Important American Weapons of World War II

Write facts about each weapon listed below. Tell why it was important during World War II.

M1 Rifle

Higgins Boat

B-17 Bomber

P-51 Fighter

Aircraft Carrier

Sherman Tank

These important facts in American history are brought to you by

_____

BIOGRAPHY

Answer the questions below.

THE MAN

When did he live? _____

What was his home state? _____

_____

What do we know about his early life? _____

_____

_____

What words would you use to describe him? _____

_____

THE SOLDIER

What war did he fight in? _____

What distinction does he hold? _____

_____

_____

HIS LATER LIFE

What book (written by him) and movie (starring him) tell about his combat

experience?_____

_____

This important person in American history is brought to you by

_____

Ernie Pyle was a famous American correspondent. His down-to-earth reporting gave Americans on the home front a sense of the sacrifices American soldiers were making overseas. Here, he writes about what he saw at Normandy, a few days after the D-Day invasion.

"Men were sleeping on the sand, some of them sleeping forever. Men were floating in the water, but they didn't know they were in the water, for they were dead....

For a mile out from the beach there were scores of tanks and trucks and boats that you could no longer see, for they were at the bottom of the water—swamped by overloading, or hit by shells, or sunk by mines. Most of their crews were lost.

You could see trucks tipped half over and swamped. You could see partly sunken barges, and the angled-up corners of jeeps, and small landing crafts half submerged. And at low tide you could still see those vicious six-pronged iron snares that helped snag and wreck them.

On the beach itself, high and dry, were all kinds of wrecked vehicles. There were tanks that had only just made the beach before being knocked out. There were jeeps that had burned to a dull gray....

On the beach lay, expended, sufficient men and mechanism for a small war. They were gone forever now. And yet we could afford it.

We could afford it because we were on, we had our toehold, and behind us there were such enormous replacements for this wreckage on the beach that you could hardly conceive of their sum total. Men and equipment were flowing from England in such a gigantic stream that it made the waste on the beachhead seem like nothing at all, really nothing at all....

And standing out there on the water beyond all this wreckage was the greatest armada man has ever seen. You simply could not believe the gigantic collection of ships that lay out there waiting to unload.

Looking from the bluff, it lay thick and clear to the far horizon of the sea and on beyond, and it spread out to the sides and was miles wide. Its utter enormity would move the hardest man.

As I stood up there I noticed a group of freshly taken German prisoners standing nearby....

The prisoners too were looking out to sea—the same bit of sea that for months and years had been so safely empty before their gaze. Now they stood staring almost as if in a trance.

They didn't say a word to each other. They didn't need to. The expression on their faces was something forever unforgettable. In it was the final horrified acceptance of their doom.

If only all Germans could have had the rich experience of standing on the bluff and looking out across the water and seeing what their compatriots saw."

What did Pyle mean by "we could afford it"? _____

_____

What made Normandy a "toehold"? _____

_____

This important person in American history is brought to you by

_____

★ 1945 ★ The End of the War and the Beginning of the Nuclear Age

Complete the fact sheet below.

FACT SHEET: THE ATOMIC BOMB

Name of the Project That Developed It: _____

Where It Was Dropped: _____

_____

Date It Was First Dropped: _____

Name of the Aircraft That Dropped the First Atomic Bomb:_____

_____

Effects on the War With Japan: _____

_____

This important date in American history is brought to you by

_____

Timeline markings (left): 1900, 1910, 1920, 1930, 1940, 1950, 1960, 1970, 1980, 1990, 2000

Timeline markings (right): 2000, 1990, 1980, 1970, 1960, 1950, 1940, 1930, 1920, 1910, 1900

★1945★ Major Effects of World War II

World War II was the greatest conflict the world has ever seen. It was truly a world war; 59 countries participated, and battles were fought on the land, at sea, and in the air all over the globe. As many as 60 million soldiers and civilians died during the war. Trillions of dollars of property was destroyed. This massive conflict reshaped the world. Complete the diagram below to show how much World War II changed the world.

World War II

Major Effect

____

____

____

____

____

____

Major Effect

____

____

____

____

____

____

Major Effect

____

____

____

____

____

____

Major Effect

____

____

____

____

____

____

This important date in American history is brought to you by

____

★1945★ The United Nations

Complete the chart below.

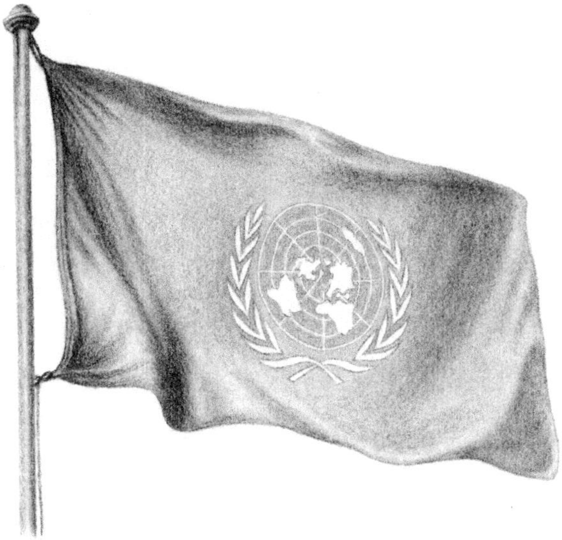

The United Nations

Purpose	
When Founded	
Location of Headquarters	
Six Major Organs	
Permanent Security Council Members	

This important date in American history is brought to you by

____

Label the following items on the map below: states in 1950, several major cities, and major bodies of water.

Fill in the missing information below. Record the total population, and shade the circle graph to illustrate the rural/urban distribution.

THE UNITED STATES IN 1950

Total Population: _____

Rural/Urban Distribution: _____

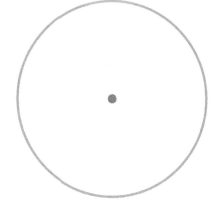

This important date in American history is brought to you by

_____

Activate the Time Machine to learn about shopping during the 1940s. In the left-hand circle, write facts about shopping during that time. In the right-hand circle, write facts about shopping today. In the space where the circles overlap, write facts about shopping that both time periods have in common.

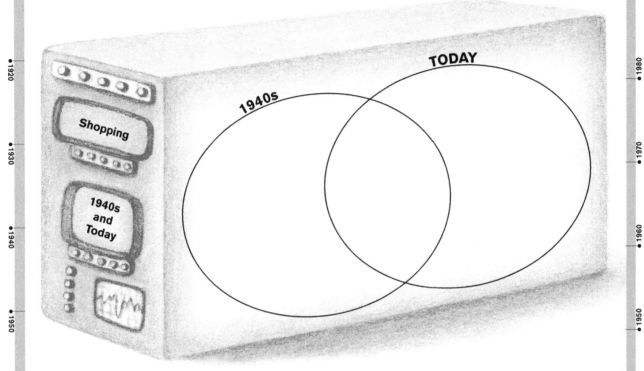

During the 1940s, a majority of Americans lived in urban areas. People made weekly, and sometimes daily, trips to stores to purchase the things they needed and wanted.

Larger towns and cities had department stores downtown, where different departments sold different types of goods, such as clothing and housewares.

More specific needs were met by going to specific stores. People purchased baked goods at the bakery, hardware at the hardware store, and recorded music at the record store. And, of course, people bought groceries at the grocery store, where items were placed in old cardboard boxes for the trip home. Gasoline was purchased at service stations, where attendants would pump the gas. They would also "check under the hood" for free. There were no suburban shopping malls or "big box" retailers.

During the war years, shopping was greatly affected by rationing. Consumers were issued ration coupons in order to limit their purchases of vital goods, like gasoline, that were needed for the war effort.

This important trip into American history is brought to you by

_____

★ The National World War II Memorial ★

The National World War II Memorial stands in the nation's capital, Washington, D.C. It "commemorates the sacrifice and celebrates the victory of the World War II generation." What is it like to visit there? Conduct research to find out.

Use the Internet or any other resources your teacher suggests. Read the articles and study the illustrations. When you have gathered enough information, make a postcard.

On the front of the postcard, draw a picture or attach a picture from a magazine or the Internet that gives some information about the National World War II Memorial. On the back of the postcard, write a caption that explains the picture. Then, write a note to a friend that tells about things to do and see at the site.

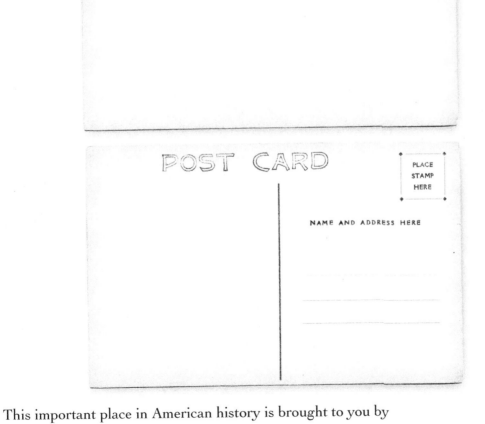

POST CARD

PLACE
STAMP
HERE

NAME AND ADDRESS HERE

This important place in American history is brought to you by

1940–1990

UNIT OVERVIEW

The Cold War was arguably the most important development during the last half of the twentieth century. This is simply because historians now recognize that the world came incredibly close to nuclear war, especially during the Cuban Missile Crisis.

This war was important for other reasons too. It shaped virtually all significant foreign policy decisions. It also cost a mind-boggling amount of money (with a corresponding, equally huge opportunity cost). In addition, the Cold War resulted in "hot spot" wars like those in Korea and Vietnam, led to revolutions, and generally kept much of the world's population in a heightened state of anxiety for many years.

Activity Sheet 7-A provides a unit overview. Activity Sheet 7-B sets the postwar stage, with American soldiers returning from World War II. By this time, the relationship between the United States and the Soviet Union—allies during World War II—was already souring.

Activity Sheets 7-C and 7-D provide essential information about the main players in the Cold War and their allies. On Activity Sheet 7-E, the students compare and contrast capitalism and communism. Activity Sheet 7-F reminds the students of the quintessential foreign policy of the United States during the Cold War: the Truman Doctrine, which evolved into containment.

Activity Sheet 7-G focuses on the arms race between the United States and the Soviet Union. Activity Sheet 7-H highlights the major developments of the Cold War, and Activity Sheets 7-I through 7-K examine three of these events: the Korean War, the Cuban Missile Crisis, and the Vietnam War. Activity Sheet 7-L provides a biography of Lyndon Baines Johnson.

The end of the Cold War comes in sight with Activity Sheet 7-M, which excerpts Ronald Reagan's "evil empire" speech. The multiple causes of the conclusion of the Cold War are the subject of Activity Sheet 7-N.

The Time Machine, Activity Sheet 7-O, compares television today to television during the 1950s. A Postcard From the Past, Activity Sheet 7-P, is about the Vietnam Veterans Memorial.

FOCUS ACTIVITIES

To focus the students' attention on this period of American history, consider the following activities:

On the Brink

Point out that historians have recently learned that the world has, in fact, come perilously close to nuclear war. Ask the students what the consequences of such a war would be. Emphasize the almost unimaginable devastation that would be caused, and challenge the students to explain why national leaders could ever consider starting such a war.

Define It

Have the students explain the term "Cold War." Ask them the following questions: What type of war would be called "cold"? What does this name imply?

Revisiting Vietnam

Invite the students to share their impressions of the Vietnam War. Ask the students what they know about it. Record accurate statements on the board. Categorize them in order to outline some main facts about this unpopular conflict.

CONSTRUCTING THE TIMELINE

This unit consists of 16 activity sheets that focus on significant events, people, and places related to the Cold War. Each activity sheet is designed to, once completed, become part of a posted classroom timeline of the period covered in the unit.

The Introduction (pages VII–XIII) provides a detailed explanation of how to use the activity sheets in the classroom and suggests various ways to construct the timeline using the completed activity sheets.

You can construct the timeline any way you see fit. Use the Timeline Components (pages XVIII–XXV) to connect the activity sheets. Below are two possible timelines, constructed from the activity sheets in this unit and the Timeline Components.

Option 1: Basic Timeline

Construct this timeline to identify only the essential elements of the period.

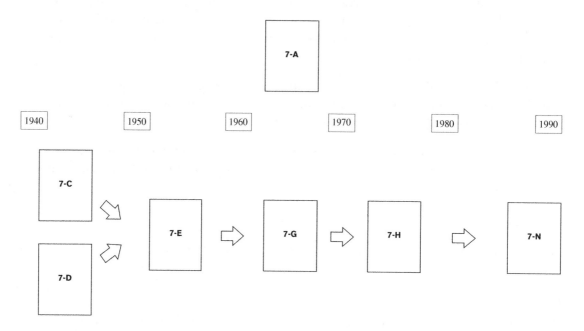

Option 2: Complete Timeline

Construct this timeline to identify the essential elements of the period, examine them in greater detail, and extend student learning.

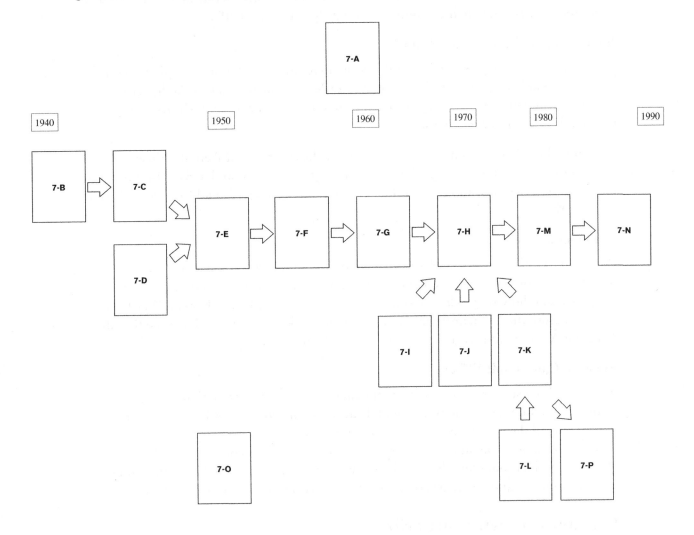

CRITICAL THINKING SKILLS

The activity sheets in this unit address various critical thinking skills. In addition, the constructed timeline emphasizes the essential critical thinking skills of identifying main ideas and details, sequencing events, and relating causes and effects.

Identifying Main Ideas and Details

Point out that Activity Sheet 7-A outlines the main ideas of the unit. Explain that the topics of the other activity sheets in the unit reflect the main ideas of the historical period the students are studying. Further explain that some activity sheets focus on the details related to specific topics.

As you and the students construct the timeline, show them that Activity Sheet 7-H forms a main idea and Activity Sheets 7-I through 7-K focus on details. Also point out that Activity Sheet 7-L discusses a detail related to the main idea addressed on Activity Sheet 7-K.

Sequencing Events

Point out that the activity sheets that make up the timeline are sequential. Show the students how the Timeline Dates provide a concrete reference for when events happened and how they relate to other events. (For example, the Korean War began in 1950 before the Vietnam War began in 1965.) Make sure the students see that the Timeline Arrows indicate a chronological flow from left to right.

Relating Causes and Effects

As you and the students construct the timeline, show them that Activity Sheets 7-C through 7-E function as the fundamental causes—superpower and socioeconomic rivalry—of all the effects that follow. The topic of Activity Sheet 7-M arguably functions as one of the multiple causes of the effect discussed on Activity Sheet 7-N. Have the students annotate the Timeline Arrows appropriately. Challenge the students to find similar relationships or create them by rearranging the activity sheets.

INDIVIDUAL ACTIVITY SHEET NOTES

The notes below provide a variety of tips on how to guide the students through the completion and extension of each activity sheet.

7-A. The Cold War

This activity is most appropriate for the students to complete with partners, in small groups, or as a whole class. For example, you might want to complete the questions with the whole class at the beginning of the unit and then have the students answer the questions at the end of the unit. Encourage the students to think of additional questions related to the topic.

7-B. Postwar America

Have the students brainstorm a list of emotions that may have been felt by Americans who were welcoming their loved ones back from the war, as well as Americans who were coming back.

7-C. The United States and NATO

Make sure the students understand that they are completing this activity sheet in order to identify essential characteristics of one of the sides in the Cold War.

7-D. The Soviet Union and the Warsaw Pact

Make sure the students understand that they are completing this activity sheet in order to identify essential characteristics of one of the sides in the Cold War.

7-E. Capitalism Versus Communism

Explain how communism, as practiced by the Soviet Union and its allied countries, was more than just an economic system. Tell the students that the communism being practiced was not the kind of communism that was originally conceived and explained. This type of communism was actually a dictatorship.

7-F. The Truman Doctrine and Containment

Point out the logic behind using the term "containment" to describe this foreign policy. Have the students evaluate containment as a foreign policy. Ask them the following questions: Was containment the right approach? If you could have dictated foreign policy in the postwar years, what would you have done?

7-G. The Arms Race

Focus the students on the fact that these were nuclear weapons and that, together, the United States and the Soviet Union built enough weapons to destroy the world several times over.

7-H. Major Events of the Cold War

You might want to re-create this activity sheet in the form of a timeline of "hot spots" during the Cold War (e.g., Korea and Vietnam).

7-I. The Korean War

Explain that the Korean War was an action of the United Nations but that the United States provided most of the money and the majority of the manpower.

7-J. The Cuban Missile Crisis

Make sure the students understand that it is no exaggeration to say that the world came very close to nuclear war during this crisis. Make sure the students know who the American President (Kennedy) and Soviet Premier (Khrushchev) were.

7-K. The Vietnam War

After the students complete this activity, quiz them by turning the headings into questions.

7-L. Biography: Lyndon Baines Johnson

Discuss Johnson's remarkable decision not to seek reelection. Emphasize the role the war in Vietnam played in his decision.

7-M. A Voice From the Past: Ronald Reagan

Make sure the students understand how controversial this type of rhetoric was; many critics thought it would increase tensions between the United States and the Soviet Union to a danger point.

7-N. The End of the Cold War

Explain that historians differ on the chief causes of the end of the Cold War; some give most credit to Reagan, others to Gorbachev, and still others to economic and social developments beyond their control. Many historians cite a combination of these reasons.

7-O. Time Machine: Television

Help the students identify the main points of the essay, which should be written in the left-hand circle of the Venn diagram.

7-P. A Postcard From the Past: The Vietnam Veterans Memorial

Suggest that the students visit www.nps.gov (the web site of the National Park Service) to gather information about the Vietnam Veterans Memorial.

In the box below, draw a picture or attach a picture from a magazine or the Internet that represents the Cold War. The picture can be of anything you think is appropriate.

Ask questions about the Cold War. Then, answer them.

Question: WHO_____?

Answer:_____

Question: WHAT_____?

Answer:_____

Question: WHERE _____?

Answer:_____

Question: WHEN _____?

Answer:_____

Question: WHY _____?

Answer:_____

Question: HOW_____?

Answer:_____

This important date in American history is brought to you by

_____

Study the illustration below. Then, write a caption for it that tells about life in the United States right after World War II. Your caption should tell about how the return of Americans from serving in the military affected life in the United States.

_____

_____

_____

_____

_____

_____

This important date in American history is brought to you by

_____

★ 1949 ★ The United States and NATO

Complete the chart below. Then, answer the question.

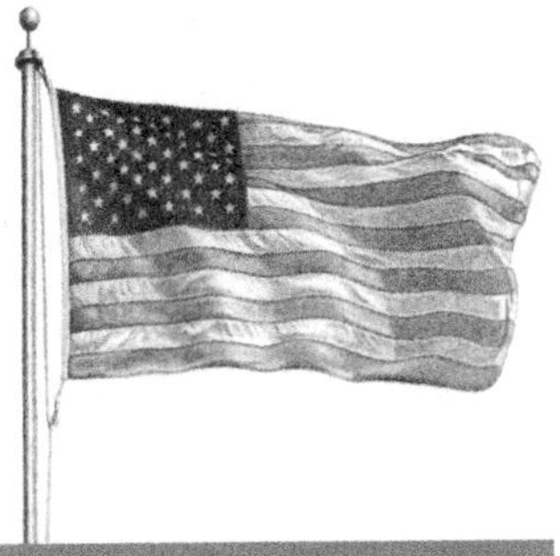

The United States	
Type of Economy	
Type of Political System	
NATO	
What It Is	
Why It Was Established	
The United States and NATO	
Relationship Between the United States and NATO	

What is the Western Bloc? ______________________________

____

____

This important date in American history is brought to you by

____

★1955★ The Soviet Union and the Warsaw Pact

Complete the chart below. Then, answer the question.

The Soviet Union	
Type of Economy	
Type of Political System	
The Warsaw Pact	
What It Was	
Why It Was Established	
The Soviet Union and the Warsaw Pact	
Relationship Between the Soviet Union and the Warsaw Pact	

What is the Eastern Bloc? _____

_____

_____

This important date in American history is brought to you by

_____

★ Beginning in the 1940s ★
Capitalism Versus Communism

Complete the diagram below. Write important facts about each system in the appropriate oval. In the space where the ovals overlap, write facts about what the systems have in common.

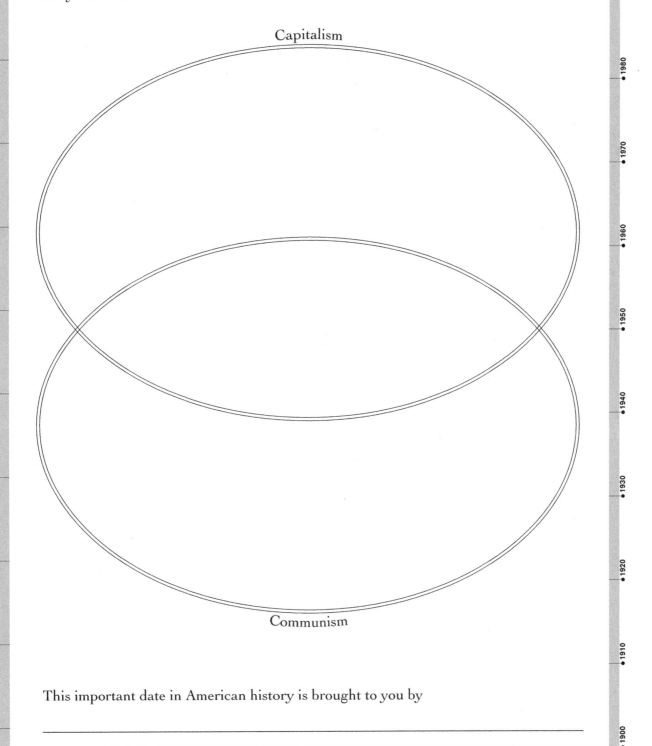

Capitalism

Communism

This important date in American history is brought to you by

_____

★ 1947 ★ The Truman Doctrine and Containment

Write two definitions below.

TRUMAN DOCTRINE

CONTAINMENT

This important date in American history is brought to you by

_____

Answer the questions below.

What was the arms race?_____

_____

Which two countries participated in the race?_____

Why did they have an arms race? _____

_____

What type of arms did they focus on? _____

_____

What were some major effects of the arms race? _____

_____

This important date in American history is brought to you by

_____

★ 1945–1990 ★ Major Events of the Cold War

Complete the timeline below.

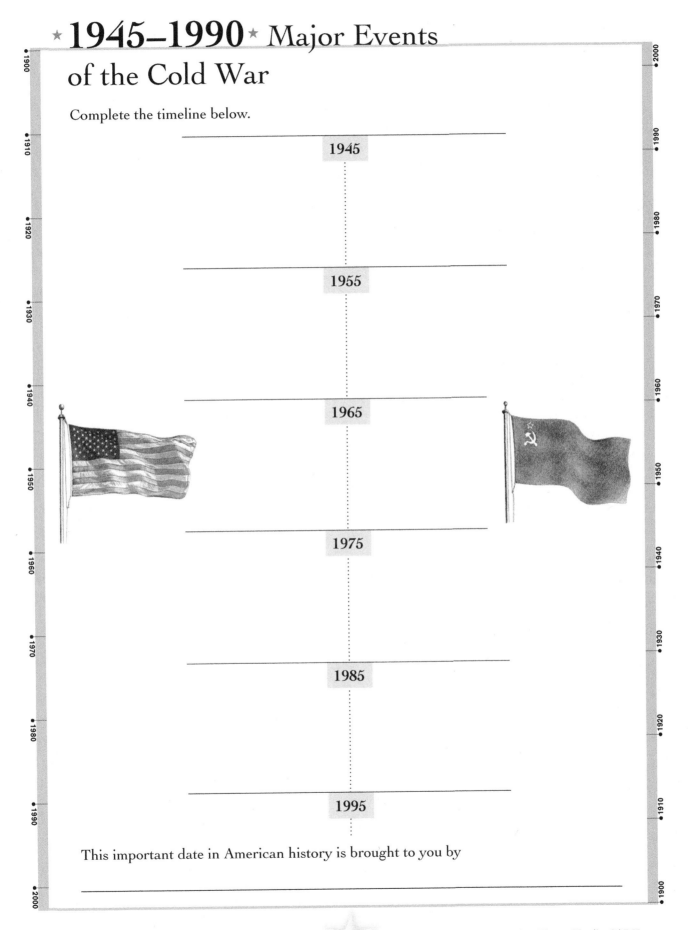

1945

1955

1965

1975

1985

1995

This important date in American history is brought to you by

Complete the diagram below.

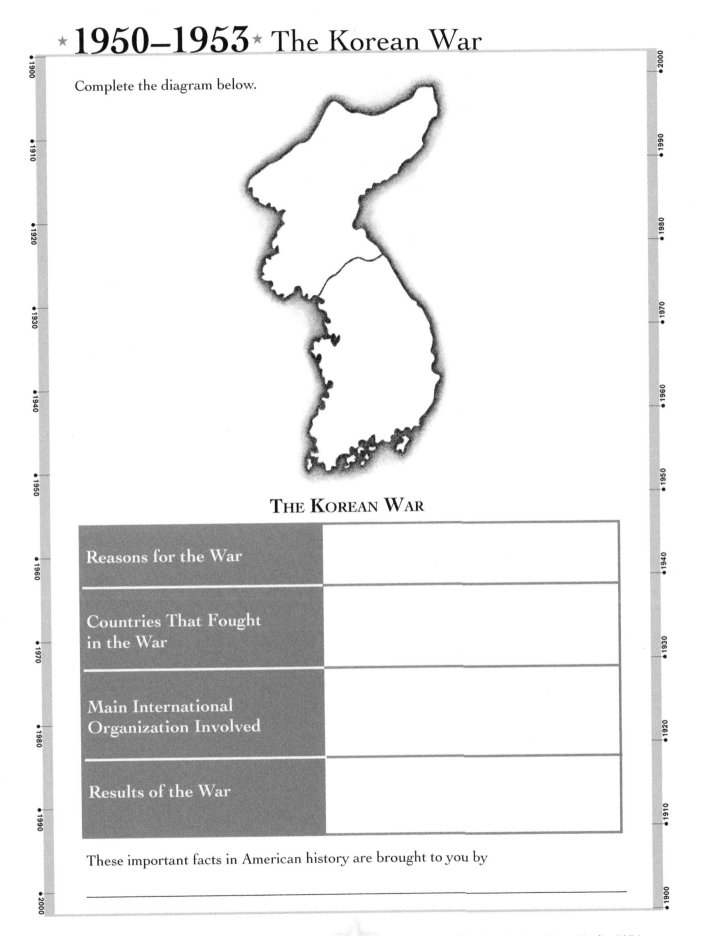

THE KOREAN WAR

Reasons for the War	
Countries That Fought in the War	
Main International Organization Involved	
Results of the War	

These important facts in American history are brought to you by

_____

Write a paragraph that tells about the Cuban Missile Crisis.

AMERICAN PRESIDENT
JOHN F. KENNEDY

SOVIET PREMIER
NIKITA KHRUSHCHEV

_____

_____

_____

_____

This important date in American history is brought to you by

_____

Complete the diagram below.

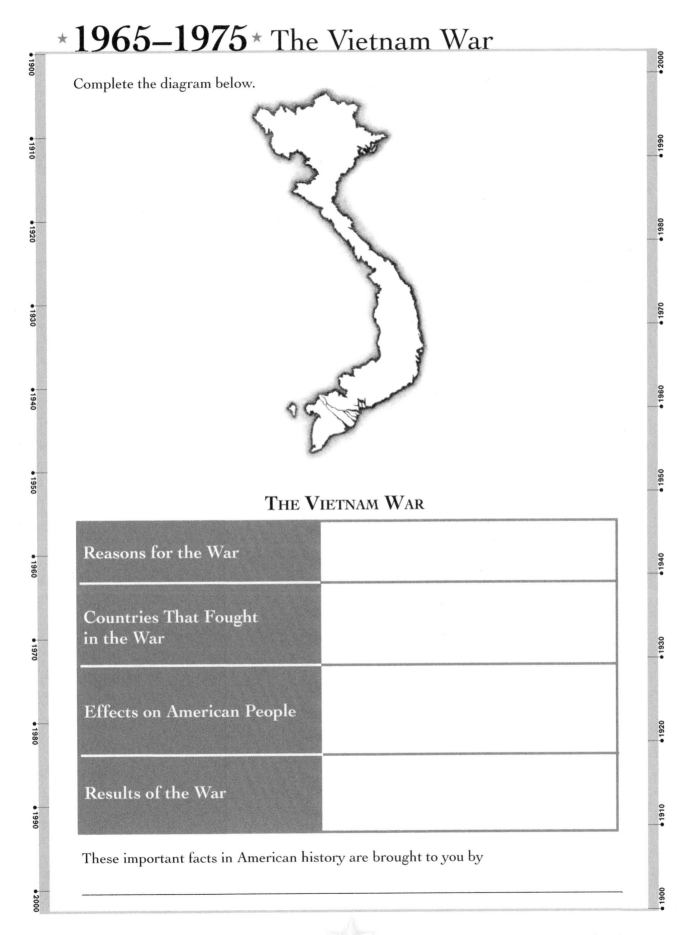

THE VIETNAM WAR

Reasons for the War	
Countries That Fought in the War	
Effects on American People	
Results of the War	

These important facts in American history are brought to you by

_____

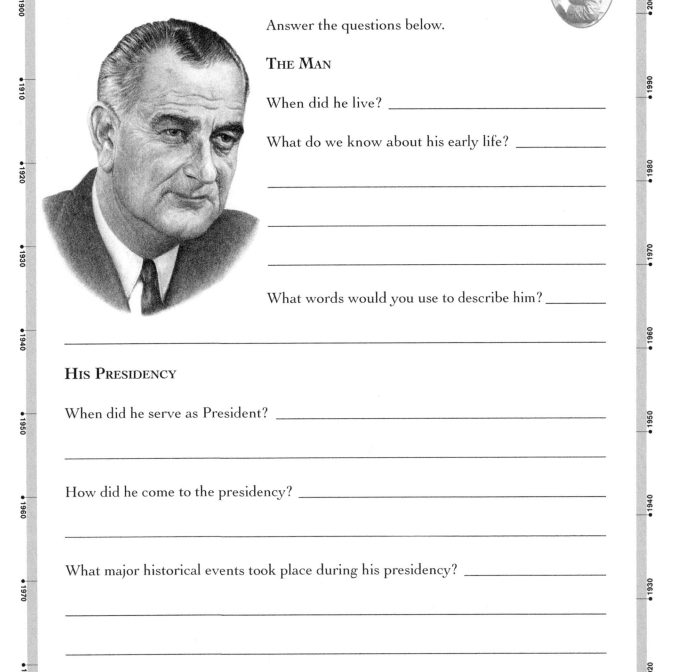

Answer the questions below.

THE MAN

When did he live? _____

What do we know about his early life? _____

_____

_____

_____

What words would you use to describe him? _____

_____

HIS PRESIDENCY

When did he serve as President? _____

_____

How did he come to the presidency? _____

_____

What major historical events took place during his presidency? _____

_____

_____

What were his major accomplishments?_____

_____

This important person in American history is brought to you by

_____

Ronald Reagan served as President of the United States from 1981 to 1989. He took a firm stance against the Soviet Union during his presidency. In 1983, he gave what has become known as the "evil empire" speech. Read the excerpt from his speech below. Then, answer the questions.

"...Especially in this century, America has kept alight the torch of freedom, but not just for ourselves but for millions of others around the world....

I intend to do everything I can to persuade [the Soviets] of our peaceful intent, to remind them that it was the West that refused to use its nuclear monopoly in the forties and fifties for territorial gain and which now proposes [a] 50 percent cut in strategic ballistic missiles and the elimination of an entire class of land-based, intermediate-range nuclear missiles.

At the same time, however, they must be made to understand we will never compromise our principles and standards. We will never give away our freedom. We will never abandon our belief in God. And we will never stop searching for a genuine peace....

Yes, let us pray for the salvation of all of those who live in that totalitarian darkness. Pray they will discover the joy of knowing God. But until they do, let us be aware that while they preach the supremacy of the State, declare its omnipotence over individual man, and predict its eventual domination of all peoples on the earth, they are the focus of evil in the modern world....

So, I urge you to speak out against those who would place the United States in a position of military and moral inferiority....I urge you to beware the temptation of pride—the temptation of blithely declaring yourselves above it all and label both sides equally at fault, to ignore the facts of history and the aggressive impulses of an evil empire, to simply call the arms race a giant misunderstanding and thereby remove yourself from the struggle between right and wrong and good and evil...."

What was Reagan's main point? _____

_____

Why did he call the Soviet Union "evil"? _____

_____

This important date in American history is brought to you by

_____

Complete the diagram below by identifying the reasons that the Cold War ended.

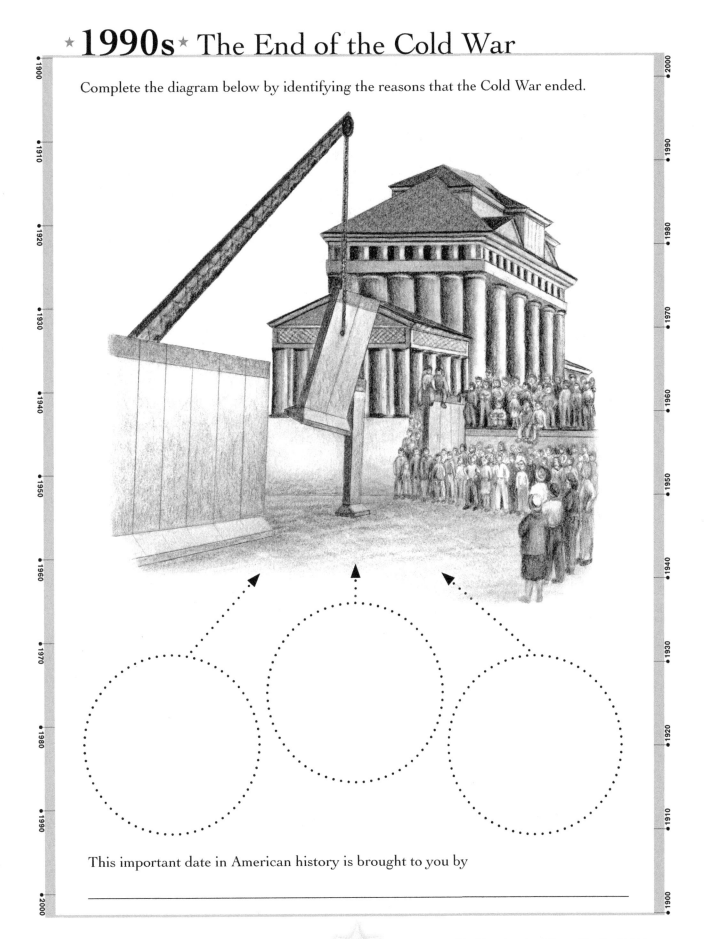

This important date in American history is brought to you by

_____

Activate the Time Machine to learn about television during the 1950s. In the left-hand circle, write facts about television during that time. In the right-hand circle, write facts about television today. In the space where the circles overlap, write facts about television that both time periods have in common.

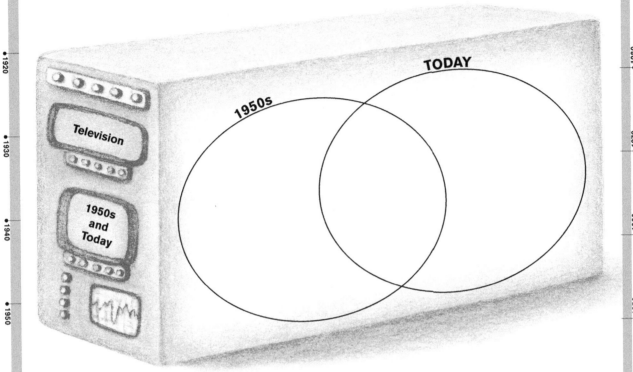

Postwar America saw a tremendous boom in television use. Only a few thousand Americans owned TVs at the time the war ended. By 1950, that amount had soared to 3.9 million. By the end of the 1950s, 46.3 million Americans owned TV sets. The 1950s saw people forgoing movies, going to restaurants, reading, and even visiting friends and family in order to be home to watch their favorite TV shows.

Situation comedies (sitcoms), like *I Love Lucy*, were among the most popular shows. Westerns, like *Gunsmoke*, and quiz shows, like *The $64,000 Question*, were also favorites. In addition, professional wrestling, comedy variety shows, and news programs were widely viewed.

At first, all shows were black-and-white. Color telecasts began in 1953. The first coast-to-coast telecast had taken place a little earlier, in 1951. All the shows were broadcast through the air. Cable was used only to bring TV signals to remote areas.

This important trip into American history is brought to you by

_____

★ The Vietnam Veterans Memorial ★

The Vietnam Veterans Memorial stands to "separate the issue of the sacrifices of the veterans from the U.S. policy in the war, thereby creating a venue for reconciliation." What is it like to visit there? Conduct research to find out.

Use the Internet or any other resources your teacher suggests. Read the articles and study the illustrations. When you have gathered enough information, make a postcard.

On the front of the postcard, draw a picture or attach a picture from a magazine or the Internet that gives some information about the Vietnam Veterans Memorial. On the back of the postcard, write a caption that explains the picture. Then, write a note to a friend that tells about things to do and see at the site.

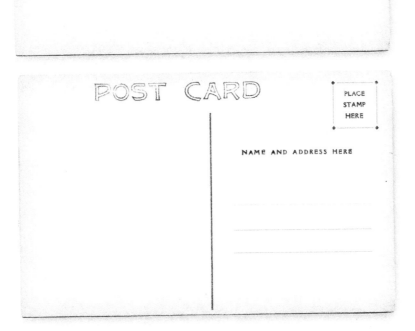

POST CARD

PLACE STAMP HERE

NAME AND ADDRESS HERE

This important place in American history is brought to you by

_____

UNIT OVERVIEW

This unit takes a wider focus than the previous units, highlighting a variety of events and developments of recent years, all of which have important effects on the students' lives.

Activity Sheet 8-A provides a unit overview. Activity Sheets 8-B and 8-C focus on one of the greatest social movements in American history: the Civil Rights Movement. The students are given an overview of the movement on Activity Sheet 8-B and a timeline of major events of the Civil Rights Movement on Activity Sheet 8-C. On Activity Sheet 8-D, the students consider excerpts from one of the most famous speeches in American history: the one given by Dr. Martin Luther King, Jr., during the March on Washington.

The next three activity sheets focus on the technology that transformed America over the past few decades. Activity Sheet 8-E is about the U.S. space program. Activity Sheet 8-F addresses the plethora of electronic consumer goods that are now a fundamental part of our economy—and consume a large share of our thoughts and income. Activity Sheet 8-G is about the Internet and the World Wide Web.

Activity Sheet 8-H provides geographic and demographic data about the United States at the dawn of the new millennium.

Activity Sheets 8-I through 8-L help the students gain perspective on the terrorist attacks of September 11, 2001, as well as America's response to them.

Activity Sheets 8-M and 8-N provide the students with the opportunities to write about their own American heroes and to identify and explain the lessons their generation should learn from studying American history.

The Time Machine, Activity Sheet 8-O, allows the students to research any subject they are interested in during any time period and compare it to the way things are today. A Postcard From the Past, Activity Sheet 8-P, is about the Civil Rights Memorial.

FOCUS ACTIVITIES

To focus the students' attention on this period of American history, consider the following activities:

"I Have a Dream"

Play a recording of the "I Have a Dream" speech given by Dr. Martin Luther King, Jr. Use the students' responses as a springboard into a discussion of the Civil Rights Movement.

An American Hero

Ask the students to identify the qualities or actions that make someone a hero. Record their responses on the board. Explain to the students that they will soon have the opportunity to identify their own great American heroes.

Current Events

Have the students monitor news sources for current news, and then have them present what they find to the class.

CONSTRUCTING THE TIMELINE

This unit consists of 16 activity sheets that focus on significant events, people, and places related to the Civil Rights Movement, technology, and terrorism during the late twentieth century through the present. Each activity sheet is designed to, once completed, become part of a posted classroom timeline of the period covered in the unit.

The Introduction (pages VII–XIII) provides a detailed explanation of how to use the activity sheets in the classroom and suggests various ways to construct the timeline using the completed activity sheets.

You can construct the timeline any way you see fit. Use the Timeline Components (pages XVIII–XXV) to connect the activity sheets. Below are two possible timelines, constructed from the activity sheets in this unit and the Timeline Components.

Option 1: Basic Timeline

Construct this timeline to identify only the essential elements of the period.

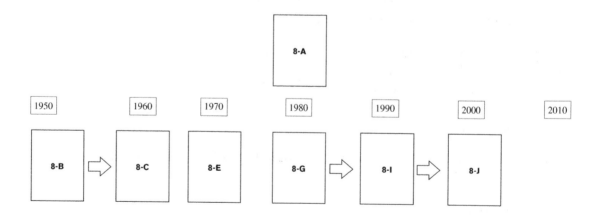

Option 2: Complete Timeline

Construct this timeline to identify the essential elements of the period, examine them in greater detail, and extend student learning.

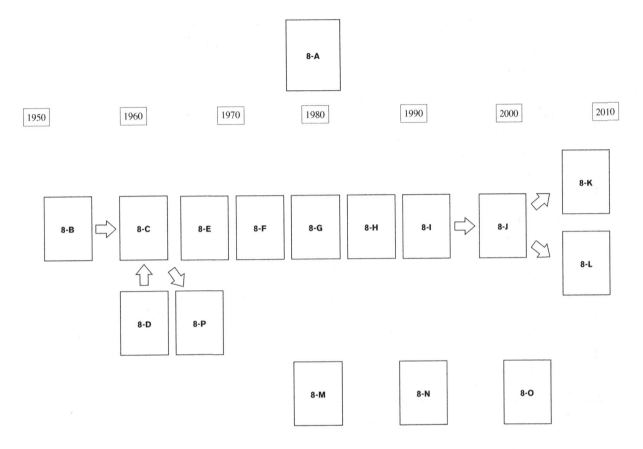

CRITICAL THINKING SKILLS

The activity sheets in this unit address various critical thinking skills. In addition, the constructed timeline emphasizes the essential critical thinking skills of identifying main ideas and details, sequencing events, and relating causes and effects.

Identifying Main Ideas and Details

Point out that Activity Sheet 8-A outlines the main ideas of the unit. Explain that the topics of the other activity sheets in the unit reflect the main ideas of the historical period the students are studying. Further explain that some activity sheets focus on the details related to specific topics.

As you and the students construct the timeline, show them that Activity Sheet 8-B forms a main idea and Activity Sheets 8-C, 8-D, and 8-P focus on details. Have the students annotate the Timeline Arrows appropriately. Challenge the students to find similar relationships or create them by rearranging the activity sheets.

Sequencing Events

Point out that the activity sheets that make up the timeline are sequential. Show the students how the Timeline Dates provide a concrete reference for when events happened and how they relate to other events. (For example, a terrorist attack was made on the United States in 2001 before Iraq was invaded in 2003.) Make sure the students see that the Timeline Arrows indicate a chronological flow from left to right.

Relating Causes and Effects

As you and the students construct the timeline, show them that Activity Sheets 8-I through 8-L form a cause-and-effect chain. Have the students annotate the Timeline Arrows appropriately. Challenge the students to find similar relationships or create them by rearranging the activity sheets.

INDIVIDUAL ACTIVITY SHEET NOTES

The notes below provide a variety of tips on how to guide the students through the completion and extension of each activity sheet.

8-A. The Civil Rights Movement, Technology, and Terrorism

This activity is most appropriate for the students to complete with partners, in small groups, or as a whole class. For example, you might want to complete the questions with the whole class at the beginning of the unit and then have the students answer the questions at the end of the unit. Encourage the students to think of additional questions related to the topic.

8-B. The Civil Rights Movement

Make sure the students understand that the Civil Rights Movement has already passed but that the fight for the civil rights of all Americans is ongoing.

8-C. Major Events of the Civil Rights Movement

You might also want to have the students list the important leaders of this movement.

8-D. A Voice From the Past: Martin Luther King, Jr.

Set the context for this activity sheet by explaining the dramatic quality and historical importance of the March on Washington. Ask an interested student to give a dramatic reading of the excerpt. Make sure the students understand that King's use of the term "negro" was not considered disrespectful at that time.

8-E. The U.S. Space Program

"Major Programs" on the diagram refers to the Mercury program, the Gemini program, etc.

8-F. New Consumer Goods

Be aware of the students' feelings as they complete this activity, emphasizing that not everyone needs, can afford, or even wants all of these goods. Explain that the point of the activity sheet is simply to illustrate an important part of the American economy.

8-G. The Internet and the World Wide Web

Take this opportunity to review appropriate school and safety guidelines for Internet use.

8-H. Map Study: The United States in 2000

Emphasize the growing population.

8-I. September 11, 2001

Invite the students to share their memories of this day, or invite an appropriate adult to share his or her experiences with the class.

8-J. The War on Terrorism

Make sure the students understand that the War on Terrorism is really a war on terrorists who intend harm to innocent citizens. Also make sure the students understand the United States' practice of holding countries that harbor terrorists equally responsible for terrorist acts.

8-K. The Afghan War

Have a pair of students conduct research and report on the current situation in Afghanistan.

8-L. The Invasion of Iraq

Have a pair of students conduct research and report on the current situation in Iraq.

8-M. Biography: My American Hero

Help the students identify the main points of the essay.

8-N. My Lessons From History

Encourage the students to identify lessons for the country, as well as lessons the students can apply in their own lives.

8-O. Time Machine: When Do You Want to Visit?

Help the students identify appropriate reference sources for their chosen topics.

8-P. A Postcard From the Past: The Civil Rights Memorial

Suggest that the students visit www.splcenter.org (the web site of the Southern Poverty Law Center, which is the sponsor of the Civil Rights Memorial) to gather information about the memorial.

★ **1954–Present** ★ The Civil Rights Movement, Technology, and Terrorism

In the box below, draw a picture or attach a picture from a magazine or the Internet that represents this period of American history. The picture can be of anything you think is appropriate.

Ask questions about this period of American history. Then, answer them.

Question: WHO_____?

Answer:_____

Question: WHAT_____?

Answer:_____

Question: WHERE _____?

Answer:_____

Question: WHEN _____?

Answer:_____

Question: WHY_____?

Answer:_____

Question: HOW_____?

Answer:_____

This important date in American history is brought to you by

_____

Complete the diagram below.

DR. MARTIN LUTHER KING, JR.

THE CIVIL RIGHTS MOVEMENT

Definition _____

_____

_____

CAUSES	ACCOMPLISHMENTS
_____	_____
_____	_____
_____	_____
_____	_____
_____	_____
_____	_____

This important date in American history is brought to you by

_____

Timeline markings (left): 1900, 1910, 1920, 1930, 1940, 1950, 1960, 1970, 1980, 1990, 2000

Timeline markings (right): 2000, 1990, 1980, 1970, 1960, 1950, 1940, 1930, 1920, 1910, 1900

Beginning in 1954 ★ Major Events
of the Civil Rights Movement

Complete the timeline below.

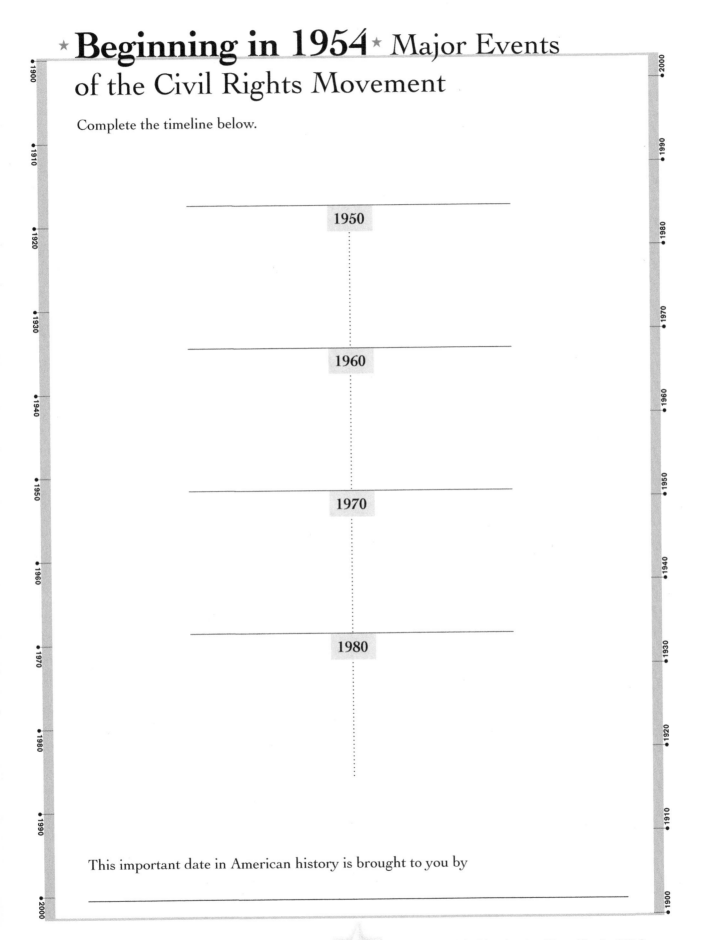

1950

1960

1970

1980

This important date in American history is brought to you by

_____

Martin Luther King, Jr.

On August 28, 1963, about 200,000 Americans joined the March on Washington to demand equal rights for African Americans. People gathered in front of the Lincoln Memorial and heard the civil rights leader Dr. Martin Luther King, Jr., give one of the most famous speeches in American history.

Read the excerpt from his speech below. Then, answer the questions.

"I am happy to join with you today in what will go down in history as the greatest demonstration for freedom in the history of our nation.

Five score years ago, a great American, in whose symbolic shadow we stand today, signed the Emancipation Proclamation. This momentous decree came as a great beacon light of hope to millions of Negro slaves, who had been seared in the flames of withering injustice. It came as a joyous daybreak to end the long night of their captivity.

But one hundred years later, the Negro still is not free. One hundred years later, the life of the Negro is still sadly crippled by the manacles of segregation and the chains of discrimination. One hundred years later, the Negro lives on a lonely island of poverty in the midst of a vast ocean of material prosperity. One hundred years later, the Negro is still languished in the corners of American society and finds himself an exile in his own land. And so we've come here today to dramatize a shameful condition....

I still have a dream. It is a dream deeply rooted in the American dream.

I have a dream that one day this nation will rise up and live out the true meaning of its creed: We hold these truths to be self-evident that all men are created equal.

I have a dream that one day on the red hills of Georgia the sons of former slaves and the sons of former slave owners will be able to sit down together at the table of brotherhood.

I have a dream that one day even the state of Mississippi, a state sweltering with the heat of injustice, sweltering with the heat of oppression, will be transformed into an oasis of freedom and justice.

I have a dream that my four little children will one day live in a nation where they will not be judged by the color of their skin but by the content of their character. I have a dream today…

And so let freedom ring–…

And when this happens, when we allow freedom to ring, when we let it ring from every village and every hamlet, from every state and every city, we will be able to speed up that day when all of God's children, black men and white men, Jews and Gentiles, Protestants and Catholics, will be able to join hands and sing in the words of the old Negro spiritual,

Free at last, free at last.

Thank God Almighty, we are free at last."

What was King's dream? _____

Has King's dream come true? Explain your answer. _____

This important date in American history is brought to you by

_____

1900
1910
1920
1930
1940
1950
1960
1970
1980
1990
2000

★ 1969 ★ The U.S. Space Program

Americans first landed on the moon on July 20, 1969. The historic event marked a high point in American space exploration, but it was by no means the first—or last—American triumph in space. Learn more about America's space program by completing the diagram below.

U.S. SPACE PROGRAM

Chief Goals	
Major Programs	
Major Accomplishments	
Famous Missions	
Famous Astronauts	
Government Agency in Charge	

These important facts in American history are brought to you by

_____

2000
1990
1980
1970
1960
1950
1940
1930
1920
1910
1900

New Consumer Goods

Many new electronic consumer products became popular in the late twentieth and early twenty-first centuries. Draw and label several of them to furnish the house and garage below.

Consider whether modern electronics are necessities or luxury items. Do they make life easier or just more complex? Explain why you think these goods have become so popular.

_____

_____

_____

_____

_____

This important date in American history is brought to you by

_____

Answer the questions below.

What is the Internet? _____

_____

What is the World Wide Web? _____

_____

What can you use them for? _____

_____

How can you access them? _____

_____

What effects have they had on American life? _____

_____

_____

This important date in American history is brought to you by

_____

Label the following items on the map below: states in 2000, several major cities, and major bodies of water.

Fill in the missing information below. Record the total population, and shade the circle graph to illustrate the rural/urban distribution.

THE UNITED STATES IN 2000

Total Population: _____

Rural/Urban Distribution: _____

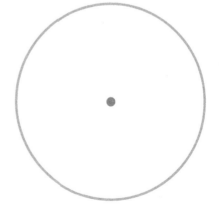

This important date in American history is brought to you by

_____

★ September 11, 2001 ★

Answer the questions below.

Who attacked the United States on September 11, 2001? _____

_____

How did they carry out their attacks? _____

_____

What were their targets? _____

_____

Why did they do what they did? _____

_____

How did the United States respond? _____

_____

This important date in American history is brought to you by

_____

The War on Terrorism

Complete the fact sheet below.

9/11

FACT SHEET: THE WAR ON TERRORISM

President Who Declared It:_____

Enemies It Is Fought Against:_____

_____

How It Is Fought: _____

How It Is Different From a Conventional War: _____

_____

_____

_____

_____

Why It Is Important: _____

_____

_____

_____

_____

These important facts in American history are brought to you by

_____

Complete the diagram below.

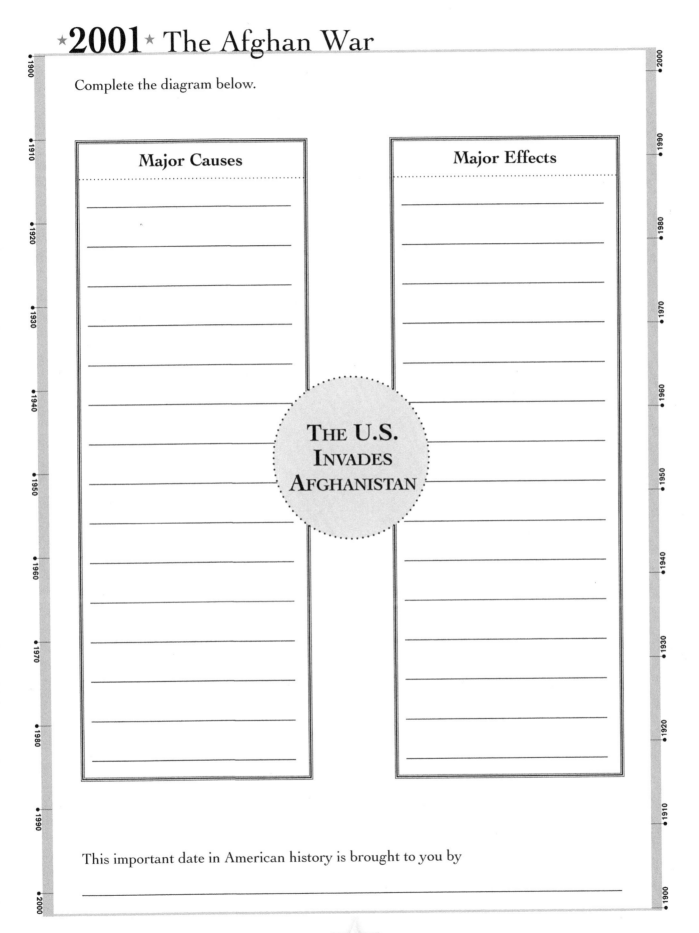

Major Causes

Major Effects

THE U.S.
INVADES
AFGHANISTAN

This important date in American history is brought to you by

_____

★2003★ The Invasion of Iraq

Complete the diagram below.

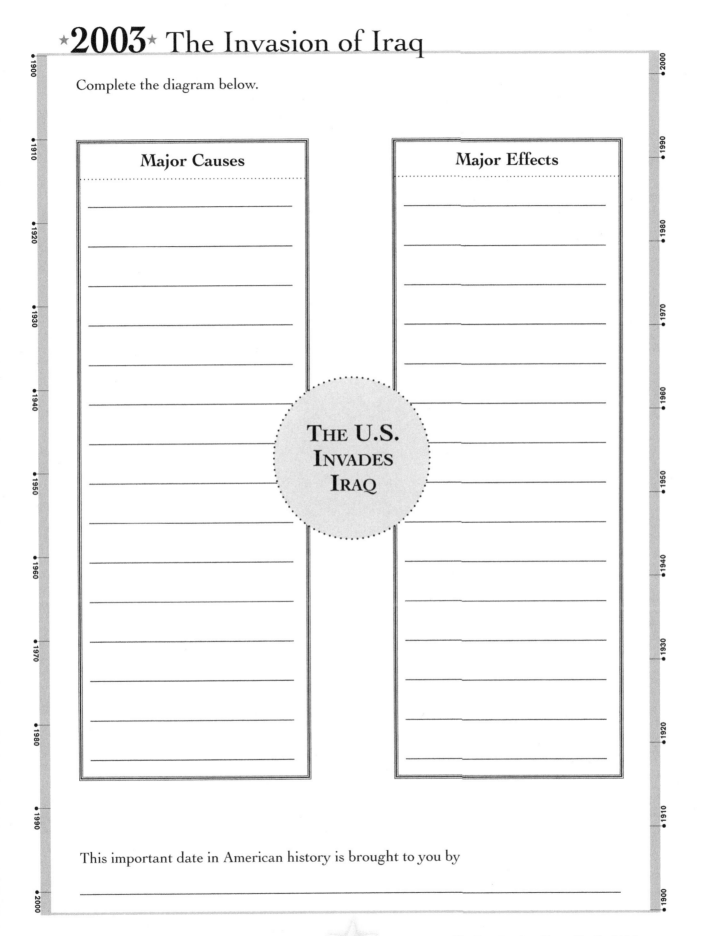

Major Causes

Major Effects

THE U.S. INVADES IRAQ

This important date in American history is brought to you by

_____

★ My American Hero ★

You have learned about a lot of famous Americans. And you surely know some Americans who, even if they are not famous, have earned your admiration.

Who is your favorite American hero? Is it someone famous from the past, or is it someone you know today? Tell about your hero by filling in the information below.

Draw a picture or symbol that represents your hero in the box.

My American Hero: _____

My Hero's Accomplishments: _____

_____

My Hero's Character Traits: _____

_____

Words Best Used to Describe My Hero: _____

_____

Lessons My Hero Has Taught Me or Others: _____

_____

This important person in American history is brought to you by

_____

Why do we study history? One reason is to avoid making the mistakes that others have made in the past. The philosopher George Santayana put it this way: "Those who cannot learn from history are doomed to repeat it." The historian David C. McCullough said, "History is a guide to navigation in perilous [dangerous] times." History, then, is perhaps our greatest teacher.

What big lessons have you learned from American history? Don't think about specific facts or dates; think about broad ideas. Write at least two of them below.

_____

_____

_____

_____

_____

_____

_____

This important lesson in American history is brought to you by

_____

Activate the Time Machine to learn about whatever you want, whenever you want. Are you curious about what music teenagers listened to in the 1980s? What about fast food in the 1950s, magazines during the 1920s, or sports in the 1900s? The list is endless. The Time Machine can take you to any subject at any time in American history.

Conduct research to activate the Time Machine. In the left-hand circle, write facts about your subject during the time you chose. In the right-hand circle, write facts about your subject today. In the space where the circles overlap, write facts about your subject that both time periods have in common.

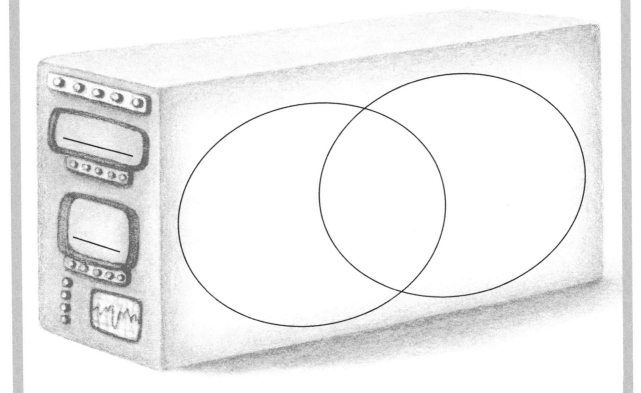

This important trip into American history is brought to you by

_____

★ The Civil Rights Memorial ★

The Civil Rights Memorial in Birmingham, Alabama, "celebrates the memory of those who died during the Civil Rights Movement," and is "a vehicle for education and reflection." What is it like to visit there? Conduct research to find out.

Use the Internet or any other resources your teacher suggests. Read the articles and study the illustrations. When you have gathered enough information, make a postcard.

On the front of the postcard, draw a picture or attach a picture from a magazine or the Internet that gives some information about the Civil Rights Memorial. On the back of the postcard, write a caption that explains the picture. Then, write a note to a friend that tells about the memorial.

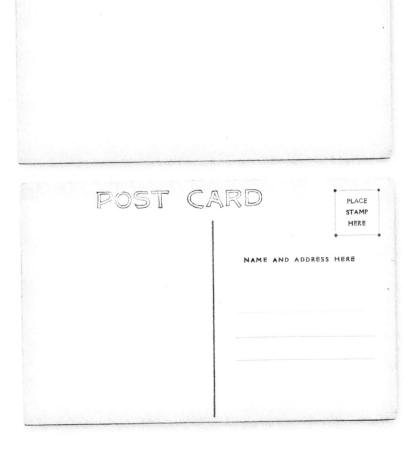

POST CARD

PLACE
STAMP
HERE

NAME AND ADDRESS HERE

This important date in American history is brought to you by

_____

★ Unit 1 ★   Assessment

Industrial Growth and Technological Advancement: 1870–1910

A. Identifying Main Ideas and Details

Match each term on the left to its description on the right. Write the correct letter in the blank.

_____ 1. Andrew Carnegie   **A.** invented the airplane

_____ 2. the Wright brothers   **B.** invented the telephone

_____ 3. Thomas Edison   **C.** made gasoline-powered automobiles

_____ 4. Duryea brothers   **D.** made a fortune in steel

_____ 5. Alexander Graham Bell   **E.** considered to be a genius

B. Sequencing Events

Number the events below to show the order in which they happened. Write the correct number in each blank.

_____ The telephone is invented.

_____ Steam power becomes important.

_____ The light bulb is invented.

_____ The airplane is invented.

_____ The modern bicycle is developed.

★ Unit 1 ★   Assessment

Industrial Growth and Technological Advancement: 1870–1910

C. Relating Causes and Effects

Write a paragraph that explains what led to the American industrial boom in the late 1800s.

_____

_____

_____

_____

_____

_____

D. Expressing an Opinion

Which invention of this period do you think is the most important? Explain your answer.

_____

_____

_____

_____

_____

_____

★ Unit 2 ★

Assessment

Big Business and Social Reform: 1870–1910

A. Identifying Main Ideas and Details

Match each term on the left to its description on the right. Write the correct letter in the blank.

_____ 1. Jane Addams   **A.** growth of cities

_____ 2. Upton Sinclair   **B.** founded Hull House

_____ 3. Statue of Liberty   **C.** formed Standard Oil Trust

_____ 4. urbanization   **D.** a gift from France

_____ 5. John D. Rockefeller   **E.** a famous muckraker

B. Sequencing Events

Number the events below to show the order in which they happened. Write the correct number in each blank.

_____ The Clayton Antitrust Act is passed.

_____ The Statue of Liberty is dedicated.

_____ Working conditions are poor.

_____ Hull House is founded.

_____ Standard Oil Trust is formed.

★ Unit 2 ★   Assessment
Big Business and Social Reform: 1870–1910

C. Relating Causes and Effects
Write a paragraph that explains why the Progressive Movement began.

_____

_____

_____

_____

_____

_____

_____

D. Expressing an Opinion
Do you think it is important for the government to regulate big businesses? Explain your answer.

_____

_____

_____

_____

_____

_____

_____

★ Unit 3 ★   Assessment
America and the World: 1867–1910

A. Identifying Main Ideas and Details

Match each term on the left to its description on the right. Write the correct letter in the blank.

_____ 1. the Great White Fleet

_____ 2. Alaska

_____ 3. Panama

_____ 4. yellow

_____ 5. Roosevelt Corollary

A. purchased from Russia

B. has a canal that connects the Atlantic and Pacific Oceans

C. based on the Monroe Doctrine

D. word used to describe inaccurate or sensational journalism

E. sailed around the world

B. Sequencing Events

Number the events below to show the order in which they happened. Write the correct number in each blank.

_____ The Alaska Purchase is made.

_____ The Spanish-American War is fought.

_____ Theodore Roosevelt becomes President.

_____ The United States takes control of Guam.

_____ The Great White Fleet sets sail.

★ Unit 3 ★

America and the World: 1867–1910

Assessment

C. Relating Causes and Effects

Write a paragraph that identifies and explains the causes and the effects of the Spanish-American War.

_____

_____

_____

_____

_____

_____

D. Expressing an Opinion

Do you think the Alaska purchase was a wise one? Explain your answer.

_____

_____

_____

_____

_____

_____

★ Unit 4 ★   Assessment

World War I: 1910–1920

A. Identifying Main Ideas and Details

Match each term on the left to its description on the right. Write the correct letter in the blank.

_____ 1. militarism   **A.** won the Congressional Medal of Honor

_____ 2. Central Powers   **B.** fought the Allies

_____ 3. Alvin York   **C.** wanted to make the world safe for
                                             democracy

_____ 4. tank
                                         D. a weapon introduced during World War I

_____ 5. Woodrow Wilson
                                         E. a cause of World War I

B. Sequencing Events

Number the events below to show the order in which they happened. Write the correct number in each blank.

_____ The Treaty of Versailles is signed.

_____ Woodrow Wilson calls for war against Germany.

_____ Archduke Ferdinand is assassinated.

_____ The home front becomes important.

_____ The League of Nations is formed.

★ Unit 4 ★

World War I: 1910–1920

Assessment

C. Relating Causes and Effects

Write a paragraph that explains why World War I broke out.

_____

_____

_____

_____

_____

_____

_____

D. Expressing an Opinion

Do you think the United States should have joined the League of Nations? Explain your answer.

_____

_____

_____

_____

_____

_____

_____

★ Unit 5 ★   Assessment

The Roaring Twenties and the Great Depression: 1920–1940

A. Identifying Main Ideas and Details

Match each term on the left to its description on the right. Write the correct letter in the blank.

_____ 1. automobiles   **A.** became popular in the 1920s

_____ 2. economic boom   **B.** policy of Franklin Delano Roosevelt

_____ 3. economic bust   **C.** a major effect of the Great Depression

_____ 4. unemployment   **D.** associated with the 1930s

_____ 5. the New Deal   **E.** associated with the 1920s

B. Sequencing Events

Number the events below to show the order in which they happened. Write the correct number in each blank

_____ *The Grapes of Wrath* is published.

_____ The Roaring Twenties take place.

_____ The nineteenth amendment is ratified.

_____ The Great Depression begins.

_____ The New Deal is implemented.

★ Unit 5 ★

Assessment

The Roaring Twenties and the Great Depression: 1920–1940

C. Relating Causes and Effects

Write a paragraph that describes some of the effects of the Great Depression.

_____

_____

_____

_____

_____

_____

D. Expressing an Opinion

Do you think the New Deal programs were the best response to the Great Depression? Explain your answer.

_____

_____

_____

_____

_____

_____

★ Unit 6 ★   Assessment
World War II: 1930–1950

A. Identifying Main Ideas and Details

Match each term on the left to its description on the right. Write the correct letter in the blank.

_____ 1. Audie Murphy   **A.** a highly decorated soldier

_____ 2. B-17   **B.** Japanese policy just before World War II

_____ 3. Ernie Pyle   **C.** a famous war correspondent

_____ 4. expansionism   **D.** an important American rifle

_____ 5. M1   **E.** an important American bomber

B. Sequencing Events

Number the events below to show the order in which they happened. Write the correct number in each blank

_____ The Japanese bomb Pearl Harbor.

_____ The Americans bomb Hiroshima.

_____ The United Nations is founded.

_____ The Allies invade Europe on D-Day.

_____ Adolf Hitler comes to power in Germany.

★ Unit 6 ★   Assessment
World War II: 1930–1950

C. Relating Causes and Effects

Write a paragraph that explains some major effects of World War II.

_____

_____

_____

_____

_____

_____

D. Expressing an Opinion

Do you think the United States was right to drop atomic bombs on Japan? Explain your answer.

_____

_____

_____

_____

_____

_____

_____

★ Unit 7 ★   Assessment
The Cold War: 1940–1990

A. Identifying Main Ideas and Details

Match each term on the left to its description on the right. Write the correct letter in the blank.

_____ 1. containment

_____ 2. John F. Kennedy

_____ 3. capitalism

_____ 4. communism

_____ 5. Ronald Reagan

A. private citizens and businesses make economic decisions

B. government makes economic decisions

C. U.S. foreign policy during Cold War

D. President during the Cuban missile crisis

E. called the Soviet Union an "evil empire"

B. Sequencing Events

Number the events below to show the order in which they happened. Write the correct number in each blank.

_____ World War II is fought.

_____ NATO is created.

_____ The Korean War is fought.

_____ The Vietnam War is fought.

_____ The Warsaw Pact is created.

★ Unit 7 ★

The Cold War: 1940–1990

Assessment

C. Relating Causes and Effects

Write a paragraph that explains why the Cold War ended.

_____

_____

_____

_____

_____

_____

D. Expressing an Opinion

Should the United States have gone to war in Vietnam? Explain your answer.

_____

_____

_____

_____

_____

_____

★ Unit 8 ★   Assessment

The Civil Rights Movement, Technology, and Terrorism: 1954–Present

A. Identifying Main Ideas and Details

Match each term on the left to its description on the right. Write the correct letter in the blank.

_____ 1. George W. Bush   **A.** declared war on terrorism

_____ 2. September 11, 2001   **B.** the date Americans landed on the moon

_____ 3. July 20, 1969   **C.** a worldwide network of computers

_____ 4. the Internet   **D.** a civil rights leader

_____ 5. Martin Luther King, Jr. **E.** the date of terrorist attacks against the United States

B. Sequencing Events

Number the events below to show the order in which they happened. Write the correct number in each blank.

_____ Terrorists attack New York City and Washington, D.C.

_____ The United States invades Afghanistan.

_____ The United States invades Iraq.

_____ The War on Terrorism is declared.

_____ Americans celebrate the beginning of the twenty-first century.

★ Unit 8 ★   Assessment
The Civil Rights Movement, Technology, and Terrorism: 1954–Present

C. Relating Causes and Effects
Write a paragraph that explains some effects of the terrorist attacks on the
United States.

_____

_____

_____

_____

_____

_____

D. Expressing an Opinion
Do you think the Civil Rights Movement has accomplished all it needs to? Explain
your answer.

_____

_____

_____

_____

_____

_____

1-A. Industrial Growth and Technological Advancement

Questions will vary, but should be relevant to the unit. Ensure answers are correct.

1-B. Map Study: The United States in 1870

Maps will vary; check for essential accuracy. Population data: 38.6 million; 74% rural, 26% urban.

1-C. The Railroad Expands

Check to ensure that data are graphed correctly. 1. A reasonable conclusion is that the railroads expanded dramatically owing to their usefulness. 2. Decreased transportation time, greater travel, economic expansion resulting from easier and faster transport of goods, increase in power of the railroad industry, western settlement.

1-D. The Strength of Steel

Steel is a strong and very useful metal made from refined iron alloyed with other metals. It largely replaced iron. Coal was needed as part of the steel-making process. The Bessemer process enabled the creation of steel in large quantities at low cost. The open hearth process improved the quality of steel. Steel was used for a wide variety of things, including railroads, buildings, and tools. It helped industry grow by providing a versatile material that was useful for goods and the tools that made them, buildings, and transportation.

1-E. Steam Powers the Nation

Steam engines were important for industrialization because industrialization requires reliable, efficient sources of power. Steam engines were used to power a very wide variety of factory and mill machines, locomotives, and farm equipment. They needed coal as fuel to heat their boilers (and to make the steel from which they were made).

1-F. American Industry Booms

Captions will vary but should indicate that the industrial boom (Second Industrial Revolution) was largely a result of abundant natural resources, new technologies (like the steam engine and factory machinery) that improved production, a growing population, and the development of new products; that important industries included the railroad, steel, and manufacturing; and that the boom made the United States a wealthier, more urbanized country.

1-G. A Voice From the Past: Andrew Carnegie

1. Perhaps because of the way it transformed the economy and landscape. 2. Answers will vary; perhaps it was not his subject or perhaps he cared little for them. 3. Answers will vary. Perhaps he is emphasizing the essential simplicity of something so important.

1-H. The Telephone

Invented by Alexander Graham Bell. First words were, "Mr. Watson, come here, I want you!" The first exchange opened in 1878 in New Haven, Connecticut. The telephone is important because it formed the backbone of a modern communications network, essential for personal, business, and government workings.

1-I. Biography: Thomas Edison

Thomas Edison lived from 1847 to 1931.

His home state was Ohio.

Words to describe Edison might include genius, hard-working, bright, curious, devoted, etc.

Things Edison invented or improved include the light bulb, motion pictures, telephone transmitter, mimeograph machine, phonograph, a vote-recorder, and stock ticker.

He invented the light bulb in 1879.

He did most of his work in Menlo Park, New Jersey.

Both quotations emphasize the importance of devoting oneself to a task.

1-J. The Bicycle

Advantages: inexpensive, simple maintenance, versatile, healthy. Disadvantages: limited speed, distance, and carrying capacity; exposure to weather. Impact on roads: riders lobbied for and achieved the building of improved roadways. Why numbers declined: increased popularity of the automobile.

1-K. The Automobile

Americans wanted automobiles for pleasure and for business. Early American auto companies included Ford, Oldsmobile, Cadillac, and Chevrolet. Major effects included increased speed and distance of transportation, migration, the building of roads, the establishment of businesses along roads, and the growth of the steel, rubber, and petroleum industries.

1-L. The Airplane

1. Orville and Wilbur Wright 2. They were bicycle mechanics. 3. Kill Devil Hill near Kitty Hawk, North Carolina 4. 120 feet; 12 seconds 5. Exhibition shows, mail transport, as observers, fighters, and bombers during World War I.

1-M. Map Study: The United States in 1900

Maps will vary; check for essential accuracy. Population data: 76.2 million; 60% rural, 40% urban.

1-N. Time Machine: American Roads

Answers will vary. Generally:

Late 1800s and Early 1900s: most were dirt, unsuitable for bicycles and cars; major expansion in the early 1900s

Today: huge network; most are paved; interstate highway system; high-tech traffic controls

Both: roads existed and were important

1-O. A Postcard From the Past: Wright Brothers National Memorial

Reward research and earnest attempts.

Unit 2

2-A. Big Business and Social Reform

Questions will vary, but should be relevant to the unit. Ensure answers are correct.

2-B. Corporations, Trusts, and Monopolies

Corporation: a business that is legally recognized as a separate entity having its own rights apart from the individuals in the business and that issues stocks and bonds

Trust: a group of corporations that cooperate to reduce competition and control prices

Monopoly: a business that has exclusive control over producing and/or selling a product

2-C. Robber Barons

1. A robber baron was a powerful business person who acquired his wealth illegally or, at best, unethically. 2. They were called robber barons after the feudal barons who would rob travelers passing through their land. 3. Major robber barons were Jay Gould, Cornelius Vanderbilt, Andrew Carnegie, J.P. Morgan, and John D. Rockefeller. They acquired their fortunes through the railroad (Gould and Vanderbilt), steel (Carnegie), banking (Morgan), and oil (Rockefeller), and the use of trusts. 4. Jay Gould, Cornelius Vanderbilt, Andrew Carnegie, J.P. Morgan, and John D. Rockefeller.

2-D. Business Corruption

Articles will vary, but should be in newspaper article format and indicate that corruption was widespread in the late 1800s. Reward research and earnest attempts.

2-E. Biography: John D. Rockefeller

John D. Rockefeller lived from 1839 to 1937.

He was born in Richford, New York.

Words to describe Rockefeller might include hard-working, bright, generous, rich, etc.

Rockefeller was concerned with oil.

His trust was the Standard Oil Trust.

It was successful because it controlled so many aspects of the oil industry.

His company was dissolved by the United States Supreme Court.

2-F. A Wave of Immigrants

Check to ensure that data are graphed correctly and that the graph has an appropriate title.

2-G. The Statue of Liberty

1. on Liberty Island in New York Harbor 2. the French sculptor Frédéric-Auguste Bartholdi 3. the people of France 4. freedom, liberty, the promise of it in the United States, friendship between the French and American peoples 5. it represented the promise of freedom and the hope for a better life in the United States 6. overall height 301 feet, 1 inch (statue itself 151 feet, 1 inch); overall weight of 225 tons; skin is riveted copper; includes stairs and elevator; face is modeled after Bartholdi's mother; nose is 4 1/2 feet long; each eye is 2 1/2 feet across.

2-H. Urbanization

Definition: growth of cities

Causes: immigration, population growth, industrialization

Effects: include overcrowding and urban problems such as sanitation and crime

2-I. Working Conditions

Captions will vary but should indicate the horrid working conditions (long hours, low wages, dangerous machinery, use of child labor, etc.) and demonstrate an understanding of how businesses exploited the poor, especially immigrants.

2-J. The Labor Movement

The labor movement was the organization of working people in an attempt to improve their working conditions. Its goals included a shorter workweek and day, higher wages, job protection, and safety measures. Important labor leaders included Samuel Gompers and Eugene V. Debs. Major organizations included the Knights of Labor and the American Federation of Labor. Workers used strikes, sabotage, negotiation, and sometimes violence. Significant accomplishments of the labor movement included the right of collective bargaining, eight-hour workdays, five- and six-day workweeks, safety reforms, and a decrease in the use of child labor.

2-K. Government Regulation of Big Business

Interstate Commerce Act: aimed at regulating railroads

Sherman Antitrust Act: outlawed trusts and monopolies

Clayton Antitrust Act: strengthened the Sherman Antitrust Act

all: necessary to limit the power of big business

2-L. The Progressive Movement

The progressive movement was composed of many individuals and groups to improve life and society in the United States through economic, political, and social reforms. Goals of the movement included ending government and business corruption and abuses, expanded suffrage (especially to women), helping the poor, improving cities, and giving citizens a greater voice in government. The group's name means that its members wanted society to move forward, or "progress," economically, politically, and socially. Important progressive leaders included Jane Addams, Robert M. La Follette, and the muckrakers. Major organizations included Hull House and other settlement houses, unions, the Populist Party, and various community groups. To accomplish their goals, progressives wrote, lectured, demonstrated, lobbied government officials, sought office, and formed aid societies. Significant accomplishments included gaining many offices, the passage of the income tax (so the wealthy could not evade taxes), the passage of initiative, referendum, and recall laws, improved working conditions, city improvements, and direct aid to countless citizens.

2-M. A Voice From the Past: Jane Addams

1. "To provide a center for a higher civic and social life; to institute and maintain educational and philanthropic enterprises; and to investigate and improve the conditions in the industrial districts of Chicago." **2.** it was the natural (decent) thing to do; it provided a "spontaneous and vital" reward

2-N. Muckrakers

Jacob Riis: *How the Other Half Lives*, 1890, urban slums

Upton Sinclair: *The Jungle*, 1906, horrible conditions in the Chicago meat-packing industry

Lincoln Steffens: *The Shame of the Cities*, 1904, city government corruption and poor conditions

Ida M. Tarbell: *The History of Standard Oil Company*, 1904, business corruption

2-O. Time Machine: Public Transportation

Answers will vary. Generally:

1890s: trolley common; used electricity; used for commuting, errand-running, and visiting; low fares

Today: buses, trains, some trolleys; gasoline engines; used for commuting, errand-running, and visiting

Both: some trolleys; used for commuting, errand-running, and visiting

2-P. A Postcard From the Past: The Statue of Liberty and Ellis Island National Monuments

Reward research and earnest attempts.

Unit 3

3-A. America and the World

Questions will vary, but should be relevant to the unit. Ensure answers are correct.

3-B. Map Study: The Alaska Purchase

Check maps for accuracy.

Area: 586,000 square miles

From Whom: Russia

How Acquired: purchase

Current State: Alaska

3-C. The Spanish-American War

Who Fought: the United States and Spain

Where Fought: the Philippines and Cuba

What Caused It: Cuban revolt, explosion of the *Maine*

Why the *Maine* Important: its destruction inflamed anti-Spanish sentiment in America

Who Won: United States

Effects: U.S. received Guam, Puerto Rico, and the Philippines; marked the United States as world power

3-D. Yellow Journalism

Definition: sensational journalism that distorts facts to create sensations and generate readership

Effects: misinformation, contributory cause of Spanish-American War, exacerbation of war fervor

Roles: rivalry between Hearst's *New York Journal* and Pulitzer's *New York World* encouraged yellow journalism

3-E. Map Study: The Hawaii Annexation

Check maps for accuracy.

Area: 6,450 square miles

From Whom: Republic of Hawaii

How Acquired: takeover orchestrated by American businesses

Current State: Hawaii

3-F. Map Study: New American Territories

Check maps for accuracy.

Guam, Pacific Ocean, none

Philippines, Pacific Ocean, none

Puerto Rico, Caribbean Sea, none

3-G. Biography: Theodore Roosevelt

Theodore Roosevelt lived from 1858 to 1919.

He led the Rough Riders in the Spanish-American War.

He was President from 1901 to 1909.

He supported "trust-busting" and conservation.

Roosevelt led the fight to have the Panama canal built.

He meant to use diplomacy but to back it up with force if necessary.

3-H. A Voice From the Past: Theodore Roosevelt

Answers will vary, but should demonstrate understanding of the essential idea of each quotation: it is better to try great things and fail than to not try at all; use diplomacy but back it up with force if necessary; protect the environment for future generations.

3-I. The Panama Canal

Location: the isthmus at Panama

Connects: Atlantic and Pacific Oceans

Why: to shorten transportation distance and times (especially for U.S. warships)

When: 1904–1913

Built By: laborers were mostly black West Indians; overseen by United States

Length: 50.72 miles

Distance saved: about 7,800 miles (from New York to San Francisco)

3-J. The Roosevelt Corollary

The Monroe Doctrine stated that the United States would not accept European expansion anywhere in the Western Hemisphere.

The Roosevelt Corollary stated that any intervention in Central and South American nations would be done by the United States and not European powers.

A doctrine is an official statement of policy.

A corollary is a rule that follows naturally from another rule.

3-K. The Great White Fleet

Captions will vary but should indicate that the Great White Fleet was a fleet of new battleships sent on a world tour by Theodore Roosevelt to demonstrate American friendship and power.

3-L. A World Power

Factors included a growing population, a growing economy, industrialization, the growth of international trade, a large navy, aggressive foreign policies, victory in the Spanish-American War, and nationalism.

3-M. Map Study: The United States in 1910

Maps will vary; check for essential accuracy. Population data: 92.2 million; 54% rural, 46% urban.

3-N. Time Machine: Journalism

Answers will vary. Generally:

1890s: sensationalism masquerading as solid journalism

Today: relatively clear line between legitimate and sensationalist news

Both: newspapers important, mix of hard and sensationalist news, people enjoy reading about crimes, accidents, and natural disasters

3-O. A Postcard From the Past: Sagamore Hill National Historic Site

Reward research and earnest attempts.

Unit 4

4-A. World War I

Questions will vary, but should be relevant to the unit. Ensure answers are correct.

4-B. War Clouds Over Europe

Militarism: build-up of armed forces made the region capable of large-scale war

Expansionism: created rivalries among European colonial powers

Nationalism: made governments especially sensitive to perceived threats or insults

Alliances: ties among countries dragged more and more of them into conflict

4-C. The Assassination of Archduke Ferdinand

Captions will vary but should indicate that Archduke Ferdinand was the heir to the throne of Austria-Hungary and that his assassination by someone with ties to Serbia gave Austria-Hungary the excuse to attack Serbia, thus starting the war; allies of each country soon joined the conflict.

4-D. The Allies and the Central Powers

Allies (major): British Empire, France, United States, Russia, Serbia (plus 19 others)

Central Powers: Austria-Hungary, Germany, Ottoman Empire, Bulgaria

4-E. A Voice From the Past: Woodrow Wilson

1. that the United States should declare war on Germany

2. German submarine warfare

4-F. Major Events of World War I

Entries will vary, but probably should at least include the assassination of Archduke Ferdinand, the United States' entry into the war, and the Treaty of Versailles.

4-G. Trench Warfare

Captions will vary but should indicate that trench warfare developed as each side built huge networks of trenches to protect soldiers from machine guns and artillery and in attempts to outflank the enemy, and that trench warfare was a gruesome business of charges across no-man's-land into enemy fire and miserable living conditions in muddy trenches.

4-H. New Weapons

Answers will vary. Essentially:

airplane: used for observation, fighting, and bombing

machine gun: rapid-fire gun that had devastating effects

tank: invented during the war as attempt to break stalemate of trenches

gas mask: for protection during poison gas attacks

4-I. The Home Front

Home Front: civilian activities that contribute to the war effort

Economic production led to the war matériel that made victory possible, an economic upswing, and more women in the workforce (as they took jobs normally done by the men who were serving in the armed forces)

4-J. The Treaty of Versailles

Major provisions included: taking territory from the Central Powers, taking weapons from them, forcing them to pay reparations, making Germany accept the blame for the war, and limiting Germany's armed forces.

4-K. Map Study: Europe Before and After World War I

Paragraphs will vary but should indicate that the changes were dramatic and refer to a few specific changes, including the creation of new countries.

4-L. The League of Nations

What: an organization of many nations

Purpose: to preserve peace

Who: President Woodrow Wilson

Why: many Americans thought it would involve the United States in dangerous foreign conflicts

What Organization Replaced It: the United Nations (UN)

4-M. Biography: Alvin York

Answers will vary. Alvin York lived from 1887 to 1964. He wanted to stay out of the army because it violated his religious beliefs. Words to describe him might include brave, principled, religious, a marksman, etc. He fought in World War I. He earned the Congressional Medal of Honor by shooting about 25 German soldiers and forcing 132 others to surrender, single-handedly. York's accomplishment was stunning, but many other soldiers demonstrated courage.

4-N. Time Machine: Popular Songs

Answers will vary. Generally:

World War I Era: sheet-music form, family sing-alongs, patriotic

Today: electronic form (radio, CDs, and mp3s), family sing-alongs less common, patriotism a less common theme

Both: people enjoy singing and listening to music

4-O. A Postcard From the Past: The Liberty Memorial

Reward research and earnest attempts.

5-A. The Roaring Twenties and the Great Depression

Questions will vary, but should be relevant to the unit. Ensure answers are correct.

5-B. Map Study: The United States in 1920

Maps will vary; check for essential accuracy. Population data: 106 million; 49% rural, 51% urban.

5-C. The Economic Boom

Main causes included the growth of the automobile industry, the growth of correlated industries (steel, rubber, oil, road-building, roadside businesses), the growth of aviation, and the post-war optimism of the period.

5-D. New Consumer Goods

Drawings should include electric appliances; specific goods could include an automobile, a telephone, a radio, various electric kitchen appliances (toasters, etc.), and so on.

5-E. The Impact of the Automobile

Effects on America included more and better roads, the growth of roadside businesses and advertising, greater mobility and migration, an improved economy, booms in the steel, rubber, and oil industries, a new sense of freedom, the development of a "car culture," and so on.

5-F. The Radio and Movies

Facts will vary, but might include: Radio—became major source of news and entertainment, made people more aware of the outside world, made stars and heroes out of certain Americans; Movies—theaters in most towns, became major source of entertainment, led to development of movie industry.

5-G. New Roles for Women

Answers will vary but could include the newly won right to vote, more participation in the workforce, greater personal freedom, and improved educational opportunities.

5-H. Causes of the Great Depression

Major causes included uneven division of income, speculation, trade barriers, and credit buying.

5-I. The Great Depression

What: a severe economic downturn

When: the 1930s

Presidents: Herbert Hoover and Franklin Delano Roosevelt

Where: North America and Europe

5-J. Life During the Great Depression

Captions will vary but should indicate that the Great Depression resulted in widespread suffering (joblessness, homelessness, malnutrition, migration, family break-ups, etc.) and that people coped in various ways, from selling possessions, to migrating in search of work, to relying on the help of private charities and, later, government programs.

5-K. Map Study: The Dust Bowl

Check maps for essential accuracy. The Dust Bowl was the drought and dust storms that struck a roughly circular area including parts of Oklahoma, Kansas, Texas, New Mexico, and Colorado during the Great Depression years of the 1930s. The Dust Bowl was caused by a combination of drought, destruction of grassland, and overgrazing. It devastated farmers, making it impossible to grow crops and costing many their farms. The Okies were Oklahoma farmers stricken by the Dust Bowl, especially those who migrated west. The Dust Bowl only ended when the drought ended and farmers implemented soil conservation techniques, like planting trees as windbreaks.

5-L. A Voice From the Past: John Steinbeck

1. A Hooverville was a shantytown; a place of rough shacks erected by the homeless as living quarters. 2. Adjectives might include dangerous, poor, scary, frustrating, humiliating, desperate, and so on.

5-M. The New Deal

N: Franklin Delano Roosevelt. E: A series of government programs designed to relieve suffering during the Great Depression. W: Because the free market had failed and many people thought the government needed to take action. D: The Civilian Conservation Corps (CCC) was a program that hired young men to complete conservation projects, like planting trees and building dams. It was designed to provide jobs and improve the country. E: Social Security is the term used to refer to government payments to people in need, especially the unemployed and the elderly. A: An agency that was part of the New Deal created to bring electrification and economic improvements to the Tennessee River Valley region. L: Other New Deal programs included the Works Progress Administration (WPA), which gave people work building parks and highways, the National Recovery Administration (NRA), which set forth rules for fair business practices, and the Public Works Administration (PWA), which gave people work building bridges and schools.

5-N. Biography: Franklin Delano Roosevelt

Franklin Delano Roosevelt lived from 1882 to 1945. As a boy, Roosevelt lived a life of privilege; he attended Harvard and Columbia Law School, and soon entered politics. Roosevelt contracted polio in 1921. Words to describe Roosevelt could include hard-working, caring, intelligent, ambitious, and so on. He served as President from

1933 to 1945. The major events of his presidency were the Great Depression and World War II. His major accomplishments were the New Deal, successful leadership through most of the war, and the inspiration he gave his countrymen. His famous statement is a call to courage.

5-O. Time Machine: Women's Fashions

Answers will vary. Generally:

1920s: ready-to-wear clothes, making clothes, knee-length loose dresses, short hair, makeup

Today: ready-to-wear clothes, making clothes less common, great variety in dress and hair styles, makeup

Both: ready-to-wear clothes, makeup

5-P. A Postcard From the Past: Franklin Delano Roosevelt Memorial

Reward research and earnest attempts.

Unit 6

6-A. World War II

Questions will vary, but should be relevant to the unit. Ensure answers are correct.

6-B. Changes in Italy and Germany

Paragraphs will vary but should refer to the rise of the dictatorships, fascism, and intense nationalism and expansion in both countries.

6-C. Japanese Expansionism

Where: generally, East Asia and the Pacific (Manchuria [China], Hong Kong, Guam, Wake, Thailand, Malaya, Burma, Singapore, the Indies, the Philippines, Pacific island groups).

Why: conquest, empire-building, desire for natural resources

How: military force, surprise attacks

Who: military leaders, Premier Hideki Tojo (beginning 1941)

When: beginning 1931 (Manchuria)

6-D. Pearl Harbor

Captions will vary but should indicate that the attack was made to nullify American Pacific naval forces to enable Japanese Pacific expansion, that it was successful for the Japanese, and that the United States responded by declaring war on Japan.

6-E. World War II: Main Ideas

Main Reasons: expansionism of dictatorships of Germany, Italy, and Japan; Main Countries: Allies—United States, Union of Soviet Socialists Republics (USSR), Great Britain, and France; Axis—Germany, Italy, and Japan; Main Leaders: Allies—United States: Franklin Delano Roosevelt and Harry S. Truman; USSR: Joseph Stalin; Great Britain: Winston Churchill; Axis—Germany: Adolf Hitler; Italy: Benito Mussolini; Japan: Hideki Tojo.

Main Results: defeat of Japan and Germany (and their allies), tens of millions of military and civilian deaths, widespread destruction, huge costs, millions of refugees, beginning of atomic age, emergence of United States and Soviet Union as superpowers, the beginning of the Cold War, and independence movements.

6-F. Major Events of World War II

Entries will vary, but probably should at least include the attack on Pearl Harbor, the invasion of Normandy, the Battle of the Bulge, the dropping of the atomic bombs, and V-E and V-J days.

6-G. The Home Front

Economy: the economy boomed and was lifted out of the Great Depression

Workforce: jobs were plentiful, and many women entered the workforce

Consumers: many consumer goods were unavailable, and many others were rationed

6-H. Important American Weapons of World War II

Answers will vary.

M1 Rifle: basic personal weapon of American soldiers; tough and reliable

Higgins Boat: landing craft used for beach assaults; essential for American island-hopping strategy against Japan

B-17 Bomber: major bomber in European theater; sturdy and dependable

P-51 Fighter: excellent American fighter; protected bombers

Aircraft Carrier: first used extensively in World War II; critical to American victories in the Pacific theater

Sherman Tank: American tank inferior to best German tanks; but key element on European battlefields

6-I. Biography: Audie Murphy

Audie Murphy lived from 1924 to 1971. His home state was Texas. Murphy came from a poor farming family. Words to describe him could include courageous, brave, patriotic, and so on. Murphy fought in World War II. He was the most decorated American soldier of the war, earning more than 25 medals. He wrote and starred in *To Hell and Back.*

6-J. A Voice From the Past: Ernie Pyle

1. he meant that it was a small price to pay for the successful invasion of Europe and that it was a small amount of the huge war production 2. it was a first step into Europe and the eventual defeat of Germany

6-K. The End of the War and the Beginning of the Nuclear Age

Project: Manhattan Project

Where: Hiroshima and Nagasaki

Date: August 6, 1945

Name of Aircraft: the *Enola Gay*

Effects: convinced the Japanese to surrender

6-L. Major Effects of World War II

Effects included death and destruction, refugees, huge costs, the defeat of Japan, Germany, and Italy (and their allies), the end of the Great Depression, the beginning of the atomic age, the spread of communism into eastern Europe and the beginning of the Cold War, the creation of new international boundaries, and so on.

6-M. The United Nations

Purpose: to promote peace, security, justice, and cooperation in international relations, and to promote human rights and progress

When: October 24, 1945

Location: New York City

Organs: General Assembly, Trusteeship Council, Security Council, Secretariat, Economic and Social Council, International Court of Justice

Permanent Members: United States, Great Britain, France, Russia, and China

6-N. Map Study: The United States in 1950

Maps will vary; check for essential accuracy. Population data: 151.3 million; 36% rural, 64% urban.

6-O. Time Machine: Shopping

Answers will vary. Generally:

1940s: downtown department stores, specific stores, groceries in boxes, rationing during World War II

Today: malls, fewer specific stores, "big box" retailers, no rationing

Both: shopping important, shopping trips, specific stores

6-P. A Postcard From the Past: The National World War II Memorial

Reward research and earnest attempts.

7-A. The Cold War

Questions will vary, but should be relevant to the unit. Ensure answers are correct.

7-B. Postwar America

Captions will vary but should indicate that the return was celebrated and marked the beginning of a prosperous and relatively happy time for many, the start of the Baby Boom, the growth of suburbs, and so on.

7-C. The United States and NATO

Economy: capitalist, free market

Political System: democracy

What: the North Atlantic Treaty Organization, alliance of free nations

Why: formed as an alliance to promote freedom and counter communism

Relationship: United States the leading NATO country

Western Bloc: democratic and capitalist countries

7-D. The Soviet Union and the Warsaw Pact

Economy: communist, command

Political system: communism

What: alliance of communist nations

Why: to exert Soviet control, to promote communism to counter the West

Relationship: USSR the leading Warsaw Pact country

Eastern Bloc: communist countries

7-E. Capitalism Versus Communism

Answers will vary. Generally:

Capitalism: economic questions answered by individuals and businesses in a free market economy; promotes individual freedom

Communism: economic questions answered by the government in a command economy; promotes state power

Both: economic system that answers the economic questions (What will be produced? How will it be produced? For whom will it be produced?)

7-F. The Truman Doctrine and Containment

Truman Doctrine: root of containment policy; U.S. policy put forth by President Harry Truman that the United States would aid free nations in resisting communist aggression

Containment: U.S. policy of trying to contain communism, or keep it from expanding

7-G. The Arms Race

1. a competition in weapons building **2.** the United States and the Soviet Union **3.** they were rival superpowers representing capitalism and freedom versus communism and oppression **4.** nuclear arms **5.** cost, tensions, danger of war

7-H. Major Events of the Cold War

Entries will vary, but probably should at least include the end of World War II, the adoption of containment, the Berlin Blockade, the Korean War, the Cuban Missile Crisis, the Vietnam War, and the tearing down of the Berlin Wall.

7-I. The Korean War

Reasons: Communist North Korea invaded South Korea

Countries: North Korea and China; South Korea and UN allies, principally the United States

International Organization: the United Nations

Results: permanent split between North and South Korea

7-J. The Cuban Missile Crisis

Paragraphs will vary but should indicate that the Soviets attempted to place nuclear missiles in Cuba, that this action led to a U.S. blockade and a standoff, that the world came close to nuclear war, and that the U.S. prevailed in keeping missiles out of Cuba.

7-K. The Vietnam War

Reasons: U.S. assistance of democratic South Vietnam against communist rebels aided by communist North Vietnam

Countries: South Vietnam and the United States; North Vietnam and South Vietnamese rebels

Effects: widespread dissension over the legitimacy of the war

Results: communists prevailed and united north and south into a communist Vietnam

7-L. Biography: Lyndon Baines Johnson

Lyndon Baines Johnson lived from 1908 to 1973. He was from a modest family in central Texas. Words to describe Johnson could include intelligent, tough, pragmatic, persuasive, and so on. He served as President from 1963 to 1969. He came to the presidency from the position of Vice President after President John F. Kennedy was assassinated. The major event of his presidency was the Vietnam War (and the dissension it caused at home). His major accomplishments included the passage of civil rights and anti-poverty legislation.

7-M. A Voice From the Past: Ronald Reagan

1. that the United States as a force of good would continue to oppose the Soviets as a force of evil **2.** because it opposed freedom

7-N. The End of the Cold War

Answers will vary but could include the American military buildup, Soviet economic problems, and the new, more soft-line policies of Soviet Premier Mikhail Gorbachev.

7-O. Time Machine: Television

Answers will vary. Generally:

1950s: television very popular; sitcoms, game shows, wrestling, comedy variety, news shows popular, largely black-and-white at first, cable rare

Today: television very popular; many more shows, cable common, color typical

Both: television very popular; some similar types of shows popular

7-P. A Postcard From the Past: The Vietnam Veterans Memorial

Reward research and earnest attempts.

Unit 8

8-A. The Civil Rights Movement, Technology, and Terrorism

Questions will vary, but should be relevant to the unit. Ensure answers are correct.

8-B. The Civil Rights Movement

Definition: the struggle for equal rights, especially for African Americans

Causes: long-term discrimination against African Americans reached a breaking point; strong leaders emerged, the Supreme Court decision in Brown v. Board of Education of Topeka, Kansas declared segregation unconstitutional

Accomplishments: include desegregation of schools and other public places, a decrease in racism, the passage of civil rights legislation

8-C. Major Events of the Civil Rights Movement

Entries will vary, but probably should at least include the Brown decision, the March on Washington, the Birmingham demonstrations, the Montgomery bus boycott, and key pieces of civil rights legislation, like the Voting Rights and Civil Rights Acts.

8-D. A Voice From the Past: Martin Luther King, Jr.

1. that people will be treated equally as the United States lives up to its creed 2. Answers will vary; although great progress has been made, many people still face discrimination

8-E. The U.S. Space Program

Possible answers include:

Chief Goals: exploration, scientific research

Major Programs: Mercury, Gemini, Apollo, Space Shuttle, Mars Rover, satellites, etc.

Major Accomplishments: landing people on the moon, a great deal of scientific knowledge about meteorology, cosmology, etc.

Famous Missions: Apollo 11, Mars Rover, etc.

Famous Astronauts: Alan B. Shepard, Jr., Neil Armstrong, Christa McAuliffe, Guion S. Bluford, Jr., etc.

Government Agency in Charge: National Aeronautics and Space Administration (NASA)

8-F. New Consumer Goods

Drawings might include a computer, CD and DVD players, atomic clocks, GPS devices, new televisions, digital cameras, etc.

Answers will vary. Reward thoughtful responses. Essentially they are all luxury items, although computers are virtually essential. Their popularity stems from their usefulness.

8-G. The Internet and the World Wide Web

1. a worldwide network of computers 2. the part of the Internet that allows for the creation of sites 3. a wide variety of things, including e-mail, research, and entertainment 4. Answers will vary. 5. Answers will vary but might include the popularity of e-mail, new forms of entertainment, and new ways of doing business.

8-H. Map Study: The United States in 2000

Maps will vary; check for essential accuracy. Population data: 281.4 million; 21% rural, 79% urban.

8-I. September 11, 2001

1. Al Qaeda terrorists 2. by hijacking and crashing airliners 3. the World Trade Center towers in New York and the Pentagon in Washington, D.C. 4. to attack the United States for its support of Israel and its perceived oppression of Muslim peoples 5. by invading Afghanistan, where Al Qaeda was based.

8-J. The War on Terrorism

President: George W. Bush

Enemies: Al Qaeda terrorists and the countries that sheltered them

How Fought: by spying, by military force, by criminal prosecutions

How Different: it was not a fight against a single country with a well-organized army

Why: it is critical to the protection of life and liberty

8-K. The Afghan War

Causes: Al Qaeda terrorists' attacks on United States; Taliban regime in Afghanistan sheltered terrorists

Effects: defeat of Taliban regime

8-L. The Invasion of Iraq

Causes: perceived fear that Iraq under Saddam Hussein was developing weapons of mass destruction, aided terrorists, and was a threat to the United States and others

Effects: defeat of Saddam's regime

8-M. Biography: My American Hero

Reward earnest attempts.

8-N. My Lessons From History

Reward thoughtful responses.

8-O. Time Machine: When Do You Want to Visit?

Reward research and earnest attempts.

8-P. A Postcard From the Past: The Civil Rights Memorial

Reward research and earnest attempts.

Assessments

Unit 1 Assessment

A. 1. D 2. A. 3. E 4. C 5. B

B. 2, 1, 3, 5, 4

C. Answers will vary but should include abundant natural resources, new technologies that improved production, a growing population, and the development of new products.

D. Answers will vary, but should be supported.

Unit 2 Assessment

A. 1. B 2. E 3. D 4. A 5. C

B. 5, 3, 1, 4, 2

C. Answers will vary but should include that the movement was a response to societal ills, including government and business corruption, the plight of the poor, and poor working conditions.

D. Answers will vary, but should be supported.

Unit 3 Assessment

A. 1. E 2. A 3. B 4. D 5. C

B. 1, 2, 4, 3, 5

C. Answers will vary but should include yellow journalism and the explosion of the *Maine* as causes and the gaining of Guam, the Philippines, and Puerto Rico by the United States as effects.

D. Answers will vary, but should be supported.

Unit 4 Assessment

A. 1. E 2. B 3. A 4. D 5. C

B. 4, 2, 1, 3, 5

C. Answers will vary but should include the militarism, nationalism, expansionism, and alliances that colored Europe in the years leading up to the war.

D. Answers will vary, but should be supported.

Unit 5 Assessment

A. 1. A 2. E 3. D 4. C 5. B

B. 4, 2, 1, 3, 5

C. Answers will vary but should include unemployment, various human sufferings, and the implementation of the New Deal.

D. Answers will vary, but should be supported.

Unit 6 Assessment

A. 1. A 2. E 3. C 4. B 5. D

B. 2, 4, 5, 3, 1

C. Answers will vary but should include some of the following: death and destruction, refugees, huge costs, the defeat of Japan, Germany, and Italy (and their allies), the end of the Great Depression, the beginning of the atomic age, the spread of communism into eastern Europe and the beginning of the Cold War, the creation of new international boundaries.

D. Answers will vary, but should be supported.

Unit 7 Assessment

A. 1. C   2. D   3. A   4. B   5. E

B. 1, 2, 3, 5, 4

C. Answers will vary but should include the American military buildup, Soviet economic problems, and the new, more soft-line policies of Soviet Premier Mikhail Gorbachev.

D. Answers will vary, but should be supported.

Unit 8 Assessment

A. 1. A   2. E   3. B   4. C   5. D

B. 2, 4, 5, 3, 1

C. Answers will vary but should include the declaration of the war on terrorism and the U.S. invasions of Afghanistan and Iraq.

D. Answers will vary, but should be supported.

Made in the USA
Columbia, SC
28 January 2025

52880503R00222